THOUSANDS...
NOT
BILLIONS

THOUSANDS...
NOT
BILLIONS

CHALLENGING AN ICON OF EVOLUTION

QUESTIONING THE AGE OF THE EARTH

DR. DON DEYOUNG

First printing: August 2005
Third printing: May 2006

ISBN-13: 978-0-89051-441-2
ISBN-10: 0-89051-441-0
Library of Congress Control Number: 2005929397

Cover by Left Coast Design, Portland, Oregon

Printed in the United States of America

Please visit our website for other great titles:
www.masterbooks.net

For information regarding author interviews,
please contact the publicity department at (870) 438-5288.

Master
Books

A Division of New Leaf Publishing Group

This book is dedicated to a wonderful family. This includes my wife, Sally; daughters Jenny, Jorie, and Jessica; their husbands Gene, Scot, and Derrik; and grandchildren Christopher, Cari, Connor, Carly, Sydney, Avery, and Finley.

ACKNOWLEDGMENTS

Many thanks to my colleagues of the Creation Research
Society, the Institute for Creation Research, and Answers
in Genesis. Your friendship and encouragement on
writing projects are much appreciated.

Many thanks to the Institute for Creation Research
and the RATE team. It was the groundbreaking discoveries from
their eight-year RATE project (sponsored by ICR)
that made this book possible.

CONTENTS

FIGURES

TABLES

PREFACE

T his book concerns the age and history of planet earth. Just how old are its continents, mountains, seas, rocks, and fossils? Some may reply that this question has already been answered by geologists. The earth is said to be ancient, with a current age estimate of about 4.56 billion years, or 4,560,000,000 years when written out. The universe beyond the earth is assumed to be much older, going back about 14 billion years. Just where do these incomprehensible numbers come from? The earth's age is based on the radioisotope dating of rocks and meteorites, a technique developed during the last century. Age estimates for the rest of the universe follow largely from the big-bang theory. These multi-billion year time spans are sometimes called *deep time*, corresponding to deep space. Deep time refers to time scales which are much larger than those by which we define our lives. It should be remembered, however, that the existence of billions of years of history is not a certainty. Deep time is a major "icon" or symbol of evolution, a presumption which is challenged in the subtitle of this book.

Evolutionary models for life, earth, and space are questioned today by a significant group of scientists worldwide. They are convinced that the earth and the entire universe are the result of a supernatural creation event which occurred just thousands of years ago, not billions of years. This book explains some of the fascinating scientific data which supports this recent-creation conclusion.

In addition to professional scientists, there are many others who have a special interest in earth history. This refers to all of us who hold a biblical world view. That is, we accept the Bible as the uniquely inspired book given to humanity by the Creator. The Bible tells us how to live and it also reveals many details of earth history including its approximate age. The straightforward reading of Scripture describes the earth and space as just thousands of years old, not millions or billions of years. Some have attempted to resolve this time difference by inserting vast ages into the biblical creation week. However, the results are neither satisfactory nor convincing. For some readers, the initial thought may be that the time of creation is not an important issue: "I believe God created everything and it simply does not matter when it all began, whether thousands, millions, or billions of years in the past." It may be true that the age of the earth is not obviously connected to the gospel message. However, many practical and profound implications follow from one's view of the earth's age. These implications are fully explained in creationist literature (Morris, 2002).

The goal of this book is to "open the window" on the serious possibility that an ancient earth is a false and misleading assumption. In sharp contrast, the following pages present the scientific case for a recently created world. If this is true, then the conventional view of ancient earth history is grossly in error. It is readily acknowledged that belief in a young earth is a radical change from the standard teaching and writing in earth science. To grasp these contrasting views of age, consider one human generation as a basic unit of time, about 25 years.

A world 6,000 years old then spans just 240 generations. However, 4.6 billion years of time would encompass 184 million generations. The young and old views of earth history indeed stand in stark contrast. The young-earth view is confidently promoted in this book because the Bible clearly points in this direction. All scientific data, as well, can be interpreted to support a recent creation. Not every reader will agree with this conclusion, but the following chapters offer challenging evidence for serious consideration.

Introduction to RATE

I n 2003, a group of leading earth scientists met in Washington, D.C., to discuss the state of the geologic time scale. This topic concerns the history of the earth. There is general consensus on the ages of major rock strata, but the geoscientists concluded that the detailed record remained "hopelessly incomplete" (Clarke, 2003). Their recommendation was the construction of three new high-tech dating laboratories in the United States whose output could add to the database of known rock ages. This proposed multi-million dollar project is to be funded by taxpayers through the National Science Foundation.

In 1997, six years earlier, another group of scientists met in San Diego to discuss the age of the earth. Their goal was similar to the first group, that is, to clarify the chronology of earth history. However, this team sought a fundamental correction to the usual assumptions of deep time. They were skeptical of the evolutionary time scale which dominates modern geology. These scientists reviewed the assumptions and procedures used in estimating the ages of rock strata and they recognized multiple weaknesses. This group identifies itself with the acronym RATE which stands for **R**adioisotopes and the **A**ge of **t**he Earth. The seven RATE scientists include two geologists (Steven Austin, Andrew Snelling), a geophysicist (John Baumgardner), three physicists (Eugene Chaffin, Don DeYoung, Russell Humphreys), and a meteorologist (Larry Vardiman, chairman of RATE). Steven Boyd, a biblical Hebrew scholar, also joined the RATE effort. Each of the team members holds an earned doctorate.

Several research initiatives were identified and conducted over an eight-year period. The RATE project was sponsored and promoted by leading creation science organizations. These included the Institute for Creation Research and the Creation Research Society. The ministry Answers in Genesis also gave start-up support to the project. Technical research activity is expensive, and all RATE costs were covered by private donations. Sincere thanks are expressed to the many individuals and organizations which financially supported the RATE effort.

This book summarizes the RATE research and results with a minimum of technical terms. Several related references, available in many public and college libraries, are listed at the end of the book. They are indicated in the text by parentheses, for example (Morris, 2002). A comprehensive treatment of the RATE research is available in two publications. The first is titled *Radioisotopes and the Age of the Earth: A Young-Earth Creationist Research Initiative* (Vardiman et al., 2000). This volume fully explains the initial RATE research plans and also includes a comprehensive 90-page glossary of terms. The second technical book has the same main title with the subtitle *Results of a Young-Earth Creationist Research Initiative* (Vardiman et al., 2005). These two volumes give full details of the RATE research results with complete documentation.

I express thanks to each of the members of the RATE team for permission to highlight their research and to reproduce selected data, tables, and figures. All the material in this summary book is fully credited to the RATE scientists. Any errors or misinterpretations of data are my own. Specific chapters are based largely on the research of the following RATE members:

3.	Carbon-14 Dating	John Baumgardner
4.	Helium Diffusion in Zircon Crystals	Russell Humphreys
5.	Radiohalos in Granite	Andrew Snelling
6.	Fission Tracks in Zircons	Andrew Snelling
7.	Discordant Radioisotope Dates	Steven Austin
8.	Radioisotope Dating Case Studies	Andrew Snelling
9.	Theories of Accelerated Nuclear Decay	Eugene Chaffin
10.	A Proper Reading of Genesis 1:1–2:3	Steven Boyd

During the entire project there was continual positive discussion between the RATE members. All of the RATE team contributed significantly to each of the topics and chapters in this book. Many other friends also offered helpful suggestions and encouragement to the RATE effort. The project has been a positive, educational experience for all of us. We hope for similar results for those who read and study the RATE material.

Chapter 1

A Brief History of Radiation Studies

O ur story begins just over a century ago in Europe. Several scientists explored the mysterious rays given off by various mineral ores mined from the earth. These invisible rays were observed to remove a build-up of static electricity and they also caused certain materials to fluoresce or glow in the dark. The names of the science pioneers include Henri Becquerel, Frederick Soddy, Ernest Rutherford, Wilhelm Roentgen, J.J. Thomson, Marie Sklodowska Curie, and her husband, Pierre Curie. Each of these eventually received Nobel Prizes for their scientific research.

One of the minerals they studied was a variety of uranium ore commonly called *pitchblende*. It is now known as uraninite with the chemical formula UO_2. Other uranium oxides refined by chemical separation include U_2O_3, UO_3, and U_3O_8. Working in Paris, Henri Becquerel noticed in 1896 that the radiation given off by uranium compounds could fog or darken a photographic plate even when the plate was kept inside its protective cover. Unseen particles emitted by the mineral ore were energetic enough to penetrate the shielding and expose the film.

To help our understanding of the radiation particles, a brief review of chemistry is helpful. There are currently about 115 known elements in the periodic table. Not all printed tables are up to date and the most recent elements have not been verified or named as of this writing. The newer entries are made in the laboratory by colliding known elements. They have very brief lifetimes, typically milliseconds or less. Of the total known elements, 92 occur naturally, the heaviest being uranium. Most of the elements themselves also occur in several varieties called *isotopes*. The Greek roots, *iso* and *topos,* mean "same place" since all the isotopes of a given element are chemically similar and occupy the same space in the periodic table. As an example, there are three naturally occurring isotopes of the element carbon — carbon-12, 13, and 14 (Figure 1-1). These numbers are the atomic weights or masses of the isotopes compared with hydrogen, which is the lightest element. The

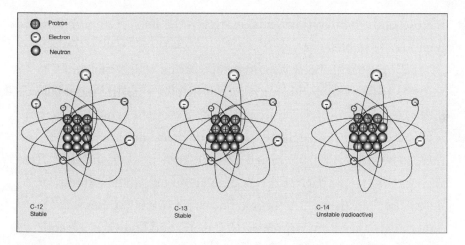

Figure 1-1. An illustration of three varieties or isotopes of the element carbon. The nucleus at the center of each carbon atom always holds six protons; the number of neutrons varies for the different isotopes. Carbon-12 and 13 are stable. Carbon-14 is unstable and radioactive with a half-life of 5,730 years.

carbon-12 atom is by far the most abundant carbon isotope and weighs 12 times as much as hydrogen. The number labels are often written as C-12, C-13, and C-14, or alternately as superscripts, for example ^{12}C, ^{13}C, and ^{14}C.

Each atom of carbon has six protons in its nucleus. The number of protons in an element is known as its atomic number. This is also the number of electrons which orbit the carbon nucleus, although electrons are often shared with other atoms by chemical bonding. Carbon-13 is slightly heavier than carbon-12 because the C-13 variety has one additional neutron in its nucleus, seven instead of the usual six neutrons of carbon-12. Isotopes which possess extra neutrons, such as carbon-14, often are unstable and eventually experience radioactive decay. In this process, the isotope radiates away energy and particles. There are more than 2,000 known isotopes among all the elements. Uranium alone has at least 28 distinct isotope varieties. The majority of all isotopes are radioactive, with a great range of lifetimes from microseconds to billions of years. However, the most common isotopes in nature are stable.

The topic of this book is radioisotope dating which concerns processes within the atomic nucleus. It is helpful to realize the small size of this central portion of the atom. The diameter of a typical atom, out to where the electrons circulate, is about one ten-billionth of a meter. This can be written as 10^{-10} meter, a length known as one *angstrom*. The thickness of a single page of this book is about one million atoms, or one million angstroms. The atomic nucleus is 100,000 times *smaller* than a single angstrom, written as 10^{-15} meter and known as a length of one *fermi* or *femtometer*. Suppose the nucleus of an atom could be enlarged to the size of a baseball. Then the outer electrons would orbit at a distance of about three miles, or five kilometers. This illustration shows that an atom is mostly empty space. The central nucleus is indeed extremely compact, even though it holds almost the entire mass or weight of the atom. Nuclear decay clearly involves the behavior of matter on the very small, sub-microscopic scale.

Early experiments revealed that radiation particles were emitted from within the atom's nucleus. It was discovered that when this occurs a very fundamental alteration also takes place: the original element becomes an entirely different kind of atom. For example, uranium atoms eventually turn into the element lead. Several centuries ago medieval alchemists attempted to change various "base metals" into gold. Today, we know that the process of radioactivity actually performs such transformations. For example, one particular isotope of mercury, Hg-190, decays spontaneously to gold, Au-190. However, this rare form of mercury is even more valuable than the few gold atoms which result from the transition.

Varieties of Radiation

Three major types of radiation have been identified in nature. Ernest Rutherford named them with the first three letters of the Greek alphabet to reflect their elusive, invisible character. In the decades following Rutherford's pioneering work, research unveiled the detailed nature of these mysterious rays. The alpha rays or particles (α) are equivalent to the nuclei (the plural of nucleus) of helium atoms. An alpha particle is a tiny bound packet containing two neutrons and two protons. It carries a double plus electrical charge because of the two positively charged protons. The beta particles (β) are single electrons which carry a negative charge. Electrons are normally bound in orbits around an atomic nucleus and thus are an integral part of every atom. There are multiplied trillions of electrons in our bodies and also in every visible object. Electrons are only called beta particles when they are free from atoms and moving at high speed. Gamma (γ) rays, the third type of radiation, are a form of high-energy electromagnetic radiation. They are a part of the light spectrum with a short wavelength and a high frequency. Gamma rays are invisible to our eyes, similar to x-rays. Light in general displays the dual behavior of both waves and particles. When characterized as particles, the "wave packets" of light, including gamma rays, are called photons. The three types of radiation identified by Rutherford have very different penetrating abilities. This and several other physical properties are listed in Table 1-1. Beyond the α, β, and γ forms of radiation there are several others that can be produced in the laboratory. These include beams of positrons, neutrons, protons, and antiprotons. Each of these has important applications in physics research, technology, and medicine.

Alpha particles are often released during the decay of the heavier radioactive isotopes such as samarium, thorium, and uranium. Beta emission occurs when a neutron within a nucleus spontaneously converts to a proton and an electron. The proton stays behind and the electron is emitted from the nucleus. Gamma rays often accompany both alpha and beta radiation. The gamma radiation provides a way for atoms to release excess energy when nuclear decay occurs.

Table 1-1. The three types of radiation commonly emitted during nuclear decay are called alpha, beta, and gamma. The + and – signs represent the electrical charge of the radiation particles. The letter c stands for the speed of light in a vacuum.

Type of Radiation	Alpha	Beta	Gamma
Greek letter symbol	α	β	γ
Electrical charge	++	-	Neutral

Typical speed
c = light speed
    = 186,000 miles/second
    = 3×10^8 meters/second
	0.8c	0.99c	c

Particle identification	Helium nucleus	Electron	Light photon
Can be stopped by…	A few inches of air	A few sheets of paper or metal foil	Inches (or feet) thickness of lead

NUCLEAR HALF-LIFE

Early studies revealed a basic property of radioactive decay called *nuclear half-life*. This is the length of time required for 50 percent of a quantity of radioactive material to disintegrate or decay away. Suppose we let an arrow represent one half-life for a radioactive material and we begin with a total of N atoms. Then the remaining or leftover amount of material will decrease as half-life increments of time pass.

$$N \rightarrow N/2 \rightarrow N/4 \rightarrow N/8 \rightarrow N/16 \rightarrow N/32 \rightarrow \dots$$

It is almost as if one keeps slicing the last piece of pie in half with an ever-smaller portion of pie always remaining (Figure 1-2). Notice that in the unusual mathematics of nuclear decay, two half-lives do not equal a whole life. Instead, the passing of two half-lives of

Figure 1-2. Portions of pie illustrate the process of nuclear decay. Beginning with a whole pie, each arrow represents the loss of half the preceding portion. After three cuttings only one-eighth of the original pie remains. The arrows also represent half-life intervals of time as an initial amount of radioactive material decays and transforms into a different element. After three half-lives have passed, one-eighth of the original number of radioactive atoms remains.

time leaves one quarter of the original number of atoms remaining. An alternate way to describe nuclear half-life is that the number of atoms decaying during any given moment is proportional to the total number of atoms available. As a result, the greater the number of radioactive atoms present, the more decays will be occurring. The half-life law eventually breaks down as the number of remaining radioactive atoms approaches zero.

The frenzy of activity occurring on the invisible, microscopic level during nuclear decay is truly amazing to consider. Marie Curie discovered and worked with the particular isotope radium-226, Ra-226. This form of radium has a half-life of 1,602 years which means that Ra-226 is relatively stable or long-lasting. Consider just one gram of pure radium-226, about the weight of a paper clip. It consists of more than two billion trillion radium atoms (actually 2.66×10^{21} atoms). Within a single fresh gram of radium, as each second passes, the number of atoms disintegrating is about 37 billion. This intense level of radiation is called one *curie* of activity. The furious pace of radiation emitted from a single gram of radium continues for many centuries with little decrease in its activity. Since radium-226 is an alpha emitter, one can only imagine the invisible cloud of alpha particles spraying outward continually in all directions from a small radium source. Exposure to this radiation can cause burns and serious damage to a person's body cells. Marie Curie was unaware of the hazards from radium and other radioactive elements during her research. She suffered from chronic radiation sickness which eventually took her life in 1934, at the age of 66.

ANALOGIES TO NUCLEAR DECAY

Nuclear decay is compared with slices of pie in Figure 1-2. Because such analogies are useful in understanding the radioisotope dating process, three additional examples will be given. First, consider an hourglass which may represent a rock specimen of unknown age (Figure 1-3). Let the sand in the top section stand for radioactive parent atoms which have not yet decayed. As they disintegrate, the resulting daughter atoms are shown by the sand accumulating at the bottom of the hourglass. As a rock ages, daughter atoms likewise accumulate within

Parent Atoms

Daughter Atoms

Figure 1-3. An hourglass illustrates radioisotope decay in a rock sample. The radioactive parent atoms and their daughter products are represented by sand grains at the top and bottom of the glass. The rate of nuclear decay is controlled by half-life, just as the rate of falling sand is controlled by the width of the neck of the hourglass.

its crystal structure. The parent isotope half-life is represented by the narrowness of the neck of the hourglass. The smaller the opening, the less the trickle of sand will be, and the longer the half-life. Although helpful, there are always limitations to analogies. For example, an hourglass is completely sealed up and can be called a closed system. No sand enters from the outside world, nor can any sand leave. However, a rock is open to the environment and can potentially exchange atoms with its surroundings. Parent and daughter atoms may enter or exit a rock at any time during its history. A second limitation of the hourglass model is that a constant amount of sand passes from top to bottom during each minute. This contrasts with radioactive decay where the number of atoms decaying during successive half-lives of time diminishes. That is, one-half of the total atoms decay during the first half-life of time and only one-fourth during the next half-life increment of time.

A second nuclear decay analogy is a lighted candle. As time passes, the length of the candle slowly and steadily decreases. The candle illustrates the uncertainty in knowing the initial amount of parent and daughter atoms present in a rock. If we observe a burning candle which

Figure 1-4. The tossing of coins is an analogy for the nuclear decay process. After each toss, the half of the coins which come up tails are removed, representing atoms which have decayed. Each coin toss illustrates one nuclear half-life. After each half-life increment of time, fewer radioactive atoms remain.

is very short, this may mean either that the candle has been burning for a long time, or else the candle was short from the beginning. A burning candle also shows behavior similar to the hourglass in shortening its length by a constant amount each minute, unlike the decreasing activity of nuclear decay.

A third analogy avoids some of the limitations of both the hourglass and candle. Consider the tossing of one hundred coins onto a table (Figure 1-4). There is an equal chance of a tossed coin showing either heads or tails, so there should result about 50 of each. Let the coins which come up tails represent atoms which have decayed, and remove them from the table. Now toss the remaining 50 coins. This time, about 25 will come up tails. Again, remove these and toss the remainder of the coins, probably leaving 12–13 heads. Each coin toss is equivalent to the elapse of one nuclear half-life. Those coins which come up heads represent atoms which have not yet decayed. Coin tossing is similar to radioactivity because during each half-life there is a 50 percent chance of an atom's decay. Just as the outcome for a tossed coin is unknown, it is also impossible to know ahead of time which atoms will decay during a particular half-life. The coin-tossing exercise eventually ends when the last coin comes up tails. Likewise the number of radioactive atoms eventually reduces to zero after many half-lives have passed.

At this point, one might ask what determines the lifetime of a particular radioactive atom. For radium-226, for example, why will one particular atom decay during the next second while an identical radium atom may last for thousands of years? The simple answer is that we do not know the reason why. Nuclear decay and its related half-life property are purely statistical, experimental concepts. The internal structure and behavior of the nucleus of the atom is one of the frontiers of modern physics understanding. The following chapter describes how nuclear decay is used to measure the ages of rock samples.

Chapter 2

OVERVIEW OF
RADIOISOTOPE DATING

THE DATING TECHNIQUE

I n 1905, Ernest Rutherford first suggested that the radioactive decay process might be useful for estimating the ages of rocks. Within months the technique was applied to various minerals, and in the following decades several isotope dating methods were developed. "Nature's clock" begins ticking when radioactive isotopes are sealed within newly crystallized igneous rocks. As the word *ignite* implies, igneous rocks form when hot, molten material cools. Melted rock is called magma while underground and it becomes lava if it reaches the earth's surface. The other two basic types of rocks, sedimentary and metamorphic, are less useful for dating since their origin is preexisting, reworked rocks. Radioisotope dating requires a measurement of the quantity of daughter atoms that result from the decay of radioactive parent atoms within the igneous rock sample. For example, the radioactive parent isotope potassium-40, K-40, decays to the daughter argon-40, Ar-40, with a half-life of 1.25 billion years. This particular decay process is called electron capture:

$$\text{Potassium-40} + \text{Electron} \rightarrow \text{Argon-40} + \text{Gamma} (\gamma)$$

Suppose a rock forms with an initial K-40 content but no Ar-40. It is then found at a later time to hold substantial argon-40 atoms. As a result, the sample might be assumed to be old. In contrast, if little Ar-40 has accumulated, the sample will be dated as young or recent. The actual sample age is based on the initial K-40 amount, its half-life, and other calibration factors. The calculated age for a single sample is called the model age. This is not necessarily the absolute, correct age of the rock. There are several assumptions to the method which are discussed in future chapters. Potassium-40 can also decay in an alternate way to the electron capture process just described. In fact, the transition from K-40 to Ar-40 occurs just 11 percent of the time. The other 89 percent of decays are of the beta decay form:

$$\text{Potassium-40} \rightarrow \text{Calcium-40} + \text{Beta } (\beta)$$

Many reactions such as this are studied in the field of nuclear physics. Table 2-1 lists the popular radioactive isotopes used in the dating technique. Most of the half-lives given in the table are in the billion-year range. These numbers, while not exact, are relatively accurate. The numerical value of nuclear half-life is a measure of the stability of a nucleus. Half-life is related to radioisotope dating but is a distinct number from the calculated ages of rock samples. Also listed in the table are some materials which are commonly dated by the particular nuclear isotopes.

Radioisotope dating is performed by many commercial and university laboratories. The experiments are highly specialized and technical in nature. One key instrument used is called a mass spectrometer. It is designed to separate charged molecules, atoms, and isotopes on the basis of their weight or mass. A small amount of sample is vaporized to a gas. Individual atoms are then counted as they travel through strong electric and magnetic fields. This is done in a vacuum chamber with extreme care taken to avoid contamination. Potassium-argon dating is the most commonly used procedure today. One reason is that potassium is abundant in many rocks and minerals. The typical cost for dating a single rock sample by measuring its potassium-argon content at a commercial laboratory is about $500 in 2005. Most of the other radioisotopes procedures are more involved and more expensive.

ISOCHRONS

There is an additional concept which is vitally important to radioisotope dating called an *isochron,* which means "equal time." An isochron is a graph of data which attempts to address three dating issues. The first issue concerns whether any daughter atoms were present in the rock when it first crystallized from magma, before any parent atoms had as yet decayed. If daughter atoms were present and are not accounted for, then the rock will have a misleading appearance of age. The second issue concerns whether or not the sample has remained a closed system during its history. If not closed, various atoms can migrate into or out of the sample over time and invalidate the age calculation. The third issue addressed by isochrons concerns the most likely computed age for a rock body, based on the statistical averaging of several radioisotope measurements.

Isochrons are utilized today in almost every radioisotope dating experiment. Their description requires a bit of detail. Consider the example isochron drawn in Figure 2-1. This figure illustrates an ideal

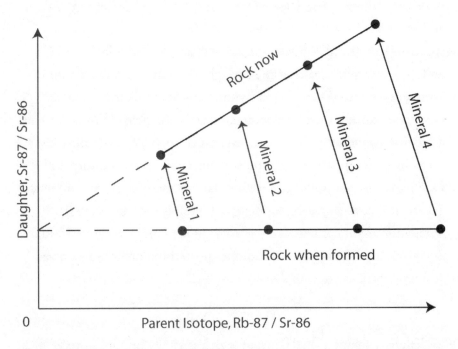

Figure 2-1. The graph is an ideal isochron which plots radioisotope data. In this example, the parent isotope rubidium-87 (Rb-87) decays to the daughter strontium-87 (Sr-87). Both amounts are divided by the strontium-86 content of the mineral samples. The black data points represent the isotope contents for four minerals taken from a rock, all of the same age. The horizontal points represent zero sample age and the sloped points occur at a later time. Isochron details are explained in the text.

THOUSANDS . . . NOT BILLIONS

case instead of actual data. Notice the quantities which are graphed. The horizontal axis records the quantity of radioactive parent rubidium-87 (Rb-87) atoms present in samples. The vertical axis measures the amount of daughter strontium-87 (Sr-87) atoms which result from the rubidium decay. Both quantities are written as fractions or ratios, with a third isotope placed in the denominator, in this case strontium-86 (Sr-86). This isotope of strontium also occurs in rock samples and is stable or non-radioactive. The reason for using ratios is that their measurement is simpler and more accurate than counting the actual number of atoms present in a sample.

In Figure 2-1 there are four black dots placed along the horizontal line. They represent the amounts of parent Rb-87 atoms in four separate minerals, all with the same Sr-87 content. Let us suppose that these four minerals come from the same igneous rock which has recently formed and has zero age. All rocks are made of one or more minerals such as biotite, feldspar, olivine, and quartz. The differing amounts of parent atoms shown by the data points arise because minerals have different affinities or attractions for each given element at the time of the mineral formation, in this case the element rubidium.

As time passes, the parent atoms of rubidium-87 embedded in the various minerals will decay to strontium-87 atoms. The line which began as horizontal will slowly tilt or rotate counterclockwise as daughter Sr-87 atoms accumulate and parent Rb-87 atoms diminish. The longer the passage of time, the steeper the slope of the line becomes. Notice that since mineral 4 in Figure 2-1 initially contains the most rubidium-87, its data point will move highest as more Sr-87 accumulates in that mineral. The Rb-87 content of all four minerals will change in tandem, or proportionally, maintaining the straight line.

In actual isotope dating procedures it is only the data points along the upper tilted line that are measured. This line, which itself is called the *isochron*, shows the measured isotope content for several minerals. The mathematical slope of the line, when properly calibrated, gives the isochron age of the sample. This age is thought to be independent of any original daughter products in the sample. In fact, the intercept point on the left side of Figure 2-1, where the two dotted lines converge, indicates the number of initial Sr-87 daughter atoms present in the minerals at the time of their formation. A least squares regression procedure is applied to the isochron line to achieve the best values for the slope and intercept. If the data points do not fall along a straight line, then one suspects open system behavior where parent or daughter atoms have moved into or out of the sample during its history.

Two distinct kinds of data can be plotted on isochron graphs. First, the parent-daughter isotope data points may come from different types of minerals separated from a single rock as just described. The resulting age is called the *mineral isochron age*. The second kind of data comes from several whole rock samples without any separation of individual minerals. The samples are taken from a single rock formation and are therefore assumed to be cogenetic. That is, they all solidified from magma at about the same time. This graph results in what is called the *whole-rock isochron age*.

An actual mineral isochron graph is shown in Figure 7-2, one of many generated for RATE samples using computer software. This isochron compares the parent isotope samarium-147 and its daughter neodymium-143. The seven data points include isotope measurements for six minerals; the rock as a whole is also plotted on the same graph. The initial amount of the daughter isotope is written as the ratio Nd-143/Nd-144 = 0.51105, taken from the left side of the graph. The mineral isochron age calculated from the slope is 1,379,000,000 years. This number is often written in literature as 1.379 Ga. The Ga stands for *Giga anna*, which is Latin for a billion years. Isochrons are assumed to be a powerful technique for assuring the accuracy of radioisotope dates. As future chapters will show, however, conflicting isochron results seriously challenge the reliability of radioisotope rock dating.

To reiterate, there are three distinct ages commonly quoted in the radioisotope literature. The model age is obtained by measuring the parent-daughter isotope ratio within a single sample. The mineral isochron age is obtained by measuring parent–daughter isotope ratios in several component minerals from a single rock sample. Finally, the whole-rock isochron age is based on parent-daughter isotope measurements for several related rock samples, all assumed to be the same age.

ARGON-ARGON DATING

In recent years, additional techniques have become popular in radioisotope dating. One is called the argon-argon (Ar-Ar) method. This is an alternate way to tell time using the potassium-argon clock. Table 2-1 lists the nuclear decay of the parent atom potassium (K-40) to its daughter argon (Ar-40). Potassium is a very common element in rocks. This includes both the radioactive isotope K-40 and also the more common stable variety K-39. This latter isotope has the nuclear property that, if the atom absorbs an outside neutron, it converts to an isotope of argon, Ar-39:

$$\text{Potassium-39} + \text{Neutron} \rightarrow \text{Argon-39} + \text{Proton}$$

In argon-argon dating, rock samples are exposed to neutrons inside a nuclear reactor to bring about this conversion. The number of new Ar-39 atoms formed is assumed to be proportional to the potassium-39 content of the sample. Since the ratio of potassium-40 to potassium-39 appears to be constant, the number of Ar-39 atoms formed is also proportional to the number of K-40 atoms in the sample.

Table 2-1 Isotopes commonly used in dating. The radioactive parent isotopes are listed along with their daughter isotopes, radiation particles emitted, half-lives, and some typical materials which are dated. Most of these nuclear decays also emit gamma rays. All the half-lives listed are the presently-measured values, written in billions of years. The value for potassium-40, for example, is 1,250,000,000 years. The initials E.C. for K-40 stand for decay by electron capture.

Radioisotope Methods

Parent Isotope	Daughter Isotope	Radiation Emitted	Half-life (Billions of Years)	Materials Commonly Dated
^{14}C Carbon	^{14}N Nitrogen	β	0.000005730 (5,730 years)	Wood, plant remains, bone, shells, glacial ice
^{40}K Potassium	^{40}Ar Argon ^{40}Ca Calcium	E.C. β	1.25	Igneous rock, minerals
^{87}Rb Rubidium	^{87}Sr Strontium	β	48.8	Igneous rock, minerals
^{147}Sm Samarium	^{143}Nd Neodymium	α	106	Igneous and metamorphic rock, minerals, lunar rock, meteorites
^{176}Lu Lutetium	^{176}Hf Hafnium	β	35	Gneiss, basalt
^{187}Re Rhenium	^{187}Os Osmium	β	43	Molybdenite ore, metallic meteorites
^{232}Th Thorium ^{235}U ^{238}U Uranium	^{208}Pb ^{207}Pb ^{206}Pb Lead	α α α	14.1 0.704 4.47	Igneous and metamorphic rock, minerals

THOUSANDS ... NOT BILLIONS

The result of the neutron bombardment procedure is that the rock sample now includes both Ar-40 and Ar-39 isotopes. A laboratory procedure is then applied to measure the ratio or fraction Ar-40/Ar-39 in the sample. The resulting number is taken as a direct measure of the sample's age since it is proportional to the daughter/parent radioisotope ratio,

$$Ar\text{-}40/Ar\text{-}39 = Ar\text{-}40/K\text{-}40$$

One major advantage of this technique is that ratios of isotopes such as argon can be very precisely measured. Also, the technique can help determine whether extra, parentless Ar-40 has entered the sample from the outside. This is important because argon-40 is by far the most common isotope of argon in the atmosphere. A final plus is that only a tiny microgram-size sample of rock is required for the analysis. As always, calibration is needed to convert the ratio to an actual age, and further assumptions also are involved.

THE LEAD-LEAD ISOCHRON

Another much-used isochron method is based solely on two stable isotopes of lead, lead-206 and lead 207. They result from the decay of the most abundant radioactive isotopes of uranium:

$$U\text{-}238 \rightarrow Pb\text{-}206 + 8\alpha + 6\beta$$
$$U\text{-}235 \rightarrow Pb\text{-}207 + 7\alpha + 4\beta$$

These decays actually go through a number of intermediate steps. Table 4-1 shows the details for the decay of uranium-238 atoms. Lead-lead isochrons are drawn based on the two lead isotopes with the amounts again written as fractions. The number placed in the denominator is the amount of Pb-204, a third isotope of lead that is not a product of nuclear decay and is present in many rock samples.

The lead-207 isotope forms faster than lead-206 because of the shorter half-life for uranium-235 (Table 2-1). The difference in lead formation times is the basis of this isochron dating method. The mathematical details of Pb-Pb isochrons may be found in technical books (Faure and Mensing, 2005). The lead-lead method was used in RATE investigations alongside the other isotope methods.

RADIOISOTOPE DATING ASSUMPTIONS

There are three basic assumptions in the radioisotope dating method. The first assumption is that the initial conditions of the sample are known accurately. This includes any daughter isotope atoms existing in rocks at their time of formation. Isochron plots may help to indicate the presence of such daughter isotopes. The second assumption is that we can tell whether or not the rock has exchanged atoms with the surroundings during its history. Isochron plots may help in determining the closed or open nature of rocks. The third assumption is that the nuclear decay rate or half-life of the parent isotope has remained constant since the rock was formed. However, if the rate of decay has changed during the rock sample's history, similar to a clock that runs either fast or slow, the calculated radioisotope age would obviously be incorrect. Isochron methods are not sensitive to testing the correctness of this third assumption.

The RATE team has found numerous examples for which the first two assumptions fail to apply. Perhaps the most significant results of the RATE project, however, relate to the third assumption, namely, the constancy of nuclear decay during the earth's past. As the following chapters explain in detail, RATE research has obtained multiple lines of objective physical evidence that nuclear decay rates have been much higher in the past than we measure today. This evidence can account for why the standard radioisotope methods often give ages in the range of millions or billions of years.

Chapter 3

CARBON-14 DATING

Research by John Baumgardner

How the Method Works

Carbon-14 is by far the most familiar radioisotope dating method. It also is distinguished from the other dating techniques because of its especially short time scale. The half-life of carbon-14 is 5,730 years, compared with millions or billions of years for the radioisotopes used in the other common methods. Also, instead of rock samples, carbon-14 dating usually is applied to the remains of once-living plants and animals — materials such as wood, charcoal, bone, shell, and fossils. The radiocarbon dating method was first introduced by scientist Willard Libby in the 1940s while he worked at the University of Chicago. Libby received the 1960 Nobel Prize in Chemistry for pioneering this important dating technique.

The formation of carbon-14, also called *radiocarbon*, is one effect of cosmic rays that constantly bombard the earth. These high energy particles from space strike molecules of gas in the earth's upper atmosphere and produce free, unattached neutrons. Some of these neutrons then combine with nitrogen-14 atoms to become carbon-14.

$$\text{Nitrogen-14} + \text{Neutron} \rightarrow \text{Carbon-14} + \text{Proton}$$

The resulting carbon-14 atoms drift downward toward the earth's surface. Along the way they combine with oxygen to make carbon dioxide molecules, or CO_2 (Figure 3-1). Living organisms, chiefly vegetation, absorb some of this carbon dioxide from the air. The CO_2 includes the stable, common isotope carbon-12 and also a tiny amount of radioactive carbon-14. There are typically a trillion carbon-12 atoms present for every single carbon-14 atom. An estimated seven kilograms of carbon-14 currently are produced in the upper atmosphere each year. This amounts to about one trillion-trillion (10^{24}) carbon-14 atoms which spread across the earth annually. Both kinds of carbon, C-12 and C-14, become part of the cellulose structure of plants and trees. Both types of carbon also enter the tissues of animals that eat the

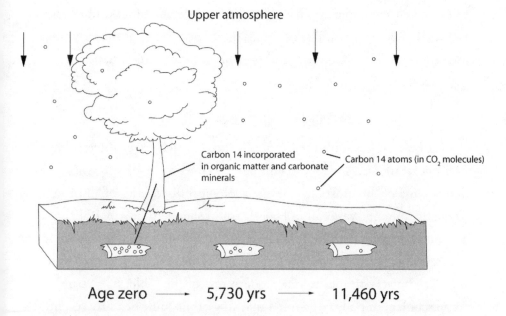

Figure 3-1. Carbon-14 atoms form several miles high in the upper atmosphere. They drift downward toward the earth's surface and combine with oxygen to make carbon dioxide, CO_2. As plants and trees absorb this CO_2, the carbon-14 atoms become a minor part of their fiber. After the vegetation dies, the internal C-14 decays away with a half-life of 5,730 years. The dots in the lower buried wood fragment represent the diminishing number of carbon-14 atoms in a sample.

plants. When the vegetation dies, it no longer absorbs carbon from the air and its trace of accumulated carbon-14 slowly decays back to nitrogen.

$$\text{Carbon-14} \rightarrow \text{Nitrogen-14} + \text{Beta } (\beta)$$

The same is true for an animal when it dies. Carbon dating involves the determination of the amount of carbon-14 remaining in the sample at a later time, usually measured as the ratio of the isotopes C-14/C-12. This value then is compared with the assumed initial carbon-14 content to estimate the sample age, based on the half-life and other calibration factors. Extreme chemical precision is essential because of the very small amount of carbon-14 present and possible carbon contamination from modern sources.

A Noted Carbon-14 Result

Carbon-14 has found many applications which are of interest to biblical studies. A well-known example concerns the Dead Sea Scrolls, one of the most famous archaeological discoveries of all time. These documents were found by a Bedouin shepherd boy in 1947. Several caves near the Dead Sea held about 800 manuscripts written in Hebrew and Aramaic. The preserved Old Testament manuscripts were found to be very similar to our modern text of the Bible. As a result, some scholars initially concluded that the scrolls must be fairly recent in age, perhaps dating from A.D. 500. However, carbon-14 dating of the linen wrappings, a plant material, showed that the scrolls were much earlier, dating between 150 B.C. and A.D. 70. This is more than 1,000 years older than other known Hebrew biblical texts. The ancient Dead Sea Scrolls demonstrate God's providence in preserving the accuracy of His Word throughout human history. Here and elsewhere in this chapter, carbon-14 is found to be a friend of biblical creation rather than a foe.

The Pervasiveness of Carbon-14

Rocks and fossils containing carbon occur in abundance throughout the earth's strata. Once living organisms now buried in these strata incorporated some carbon-14 within themselves while they were alive. For earth materials classified as ancient, all of this original C-14 content should be completely decayed away. For example, after ten half-lives of decay, any radioactive material has only 0.1 percent remaining of its original content. This small percentage results from multiplying the fraction ½ by itself ten times over. For carbon-14, this length of time, ten half-lives, is 57,300 years. If the elapsed time is extended still longer to 17–18 half-lives, corresponding to about 100,000 years, carbon-14 decays to an entirely negligible level that is undetectable by current measurement techniques. To express this in another way, any carbon-containing materials that are truly older than 100,000 years should be "carbon-14 dead" with C-14 levels below detection limits. This fact gives rise to a major challenge to the long age assumption for rocks and fossils. In recent years, readily detectable amounts of carbon-14 have been the rule rather than the exception. This is true for samples from throughout the fossil-bearing parts of the geologic record with presumed ages extending to hundreds of millions of years. The unexpected carbon-14 was initially assumed to be a result of contamination, most likely from the experimental counting procedures, but as this problem was aggressively explored, it was realized that most of the carbon-14 was inherent to the samples being measured.

Several creation scientists have previously explored carbon-14 dating, including Melvin Cook, Robert Whitelaw, Robert H. Brown, and John Woodmorappe. Also, Paul Giem conducted an extensive survey of the radiocarbon literature from the 1980s and 1990s. He found more than 70 published reports of significant amounts of carbon-14 detected in "ancient" organic samples. A further RATE review of the radiocarbon literature found many additional examples. These include carbon-14 in fossils, petrified wood, shells, whale bone, coal, oil, and natural gas. The resident carbon-14 content is also found in inorganic rocks and minerals including marble, graphite, and calcite. These samples are from all around the world and from all depths. The detected carbon-14 atoms simply should not exist in these "ancient" materials.

To understand the significance of this carbon-14 finding, consider a comparison. Suppose an archaeologist investigates an Egyptian mummy. The outer covering is carefully removed to reveal the ancient, undisturbed interior. As the last wrapping is removed an amazing discovery is made. Inside the mummy is a wind-up clock which is still ticking! Perhaps the mummy is not as old as the archaeologist initially thought. The discovery of carbon-14 in "ancient" samples is just as startling to the conventional radioisotope dating community.

Modern technology has made reliable detection of minute amounts of carbon-14 possible. In the earlier decades, the carbon-14 content in samples was measured by counting the beta radiation emitted from the few C-14 atoms which decayed in a sample during a few hours of monitoring (Table 2-1). This is a statistical process with serious limitations although it is still widely used. Since the late 1970s, a new approach became available called *accelerator mass spectrometry*, or AMS. This method allows the actual counting of individual C-14 atoms without the requirement that they decay. It is this precise AMS technique which detects carbon-14 atoms in samples at lower levels than was possible with the previous beta counting method. AMS measurements carefully eliminate all possible sources of carbon contamination. These include any trace of C-14 which has possibly entered the samples in recent history, or C-14 introduction during sample preparation and analysis. The limit of carbon-14 detection using AMS is about one carbon-14 atom for every 10^{16} stable carbon-12 atoms. This is an amazing sensitivity of one part per ten thousand trillion. It is equivalent to detecting one unique sand grain along a 100 mile-long seashore.

The presence of small amounts of C-14 in practically all carbon-bearing earth materials raises an additional concern for the radiocarbon dating method. In dating experiments, the standard practice is to count C-14 atoms in the sample and also in a "procedural blank" or calibration standard. Many laboratories use Precambrian graphite, purified natural gas, or optical grade calcite for the counting standard. This "blank" is thought to hold no C-14 whatsoever, so any counts recorded with it in place are assumed to come from the surrounding "background." These counts are subtracted from the count for the actual sample. However, we now find that the calibration blank itself may not be carbon-14–free. The counts obtained using this blank are not all coming from the background environment after all. Therefore, these counts should not be subtracted out during the sample dating procedure. The result of this incorrect counting is that many samples in past years have been carbon-14 dated older than they actually are.

RATE CARBON-14 RESEARCH ON COAL

Coal is an abundant fossil fuel consisting of buried vegetation, almost entirely composed of carbon. It is usually assumed to have formed in the distant geologic past in a swamp environment. Much coal is dated to the Pennsylvanian Period, about 300 million years ago. This is also called the late Carboniferous Period or the Age of Coal. Let us explore where geologists place the Pennsylvanian Period in earth history. Table 3-1 shows the standard geologic time scale. This is the assumed chronological sequence of rock strata, portions of which are found worldwide. The dates shown are loosely based on radioisotope results from volcanic ash and magma flows which intrude sedimentary rock layers. Notice that the Precambrian base of the time scale spans nearly 90 percent of the total assumed earth history. Above the Precambrian are fossil-bearing rock layers named Paleozoic (ancient life), Mesozoic (middle life), and Cenozoic (recent life). These three eras together are called the *Phanerozoic Eon*. This means "visible life," so named because these layers contain abundant visible fossils, unlike the Precambrian. The eras are further divided into periods such as Pennsylvanian. Table 3-1 shows this period covering the time span from 323–290 million years ago. These figures, revised slightly every few years, are taken from a 1998 Geological Society of America publication.

Table 3-1. A summary of the geologic eras, example fossil organisms, periods, and conventional time spans. The ages are taken from the Geological Society of America as of 1998. These vast time scales are not accepted by the RATE team.

Era	Representative Organisms	Period	Millions of Years Ago
Cenozoic "Recent life"	Mammals	Quaternary Tertiary	1.8–present 65–1.8
Mesozoic "Middle life"	Reptiles	Cretaceous Jurassic Triassic	144–65 206–144 248–206
Paleozoic "Ancient life"	Amphibians	Permian Pennsylvanian Mississippian Devonian Silurian Ordovician Cambrian	290–248 323–290 354–323 417–354 443–417 490–443 543–490
Proterozoic Archean (Together called Precambrian)	Bacteria, Algae	Several	4,600–543

If Pennsylvanian coal is truly hundreds of millions of years old, then no remaining carbon-14 whatsoever should be present within it. However, since the AMS method came into widespread use in the 1980s, there have been ongoing reports in the literature of traces of radiocarbon detected in coal. The RATE group further explored this possibility. Ten coal samples were obtained from the U.S. Department of Energy Coal Sample Bank, a storage site which is maintained at Pennsylvania State University. These samples were collected from major coalfields across the United States for comparative research studies. The coals are carefully preserved at low temperature in an environment of argon gas. The particular RATE samples, 300 grams each, were chosen from across the geologic span of time. They cover the Paleozoic, Mesozoic, and Cenozoic eras. These samples were analyzed for their C-14 content using the modern AMS method. The work was contracted out to one of the foremost carbon-14 laboratories in the world. Four AMS carbon-14 measurements were made for each sample and the results were averaged. As always, extreme care was taken to eliminate all possible sources of carbon-14 contamination.

Table 3-2 summarizes the RATE results for the coal samples. Also listed are the locations of the coal beds and their assumed geologic ages. The right column shows that a residue of carbon-14 atoms was found in all ten samples. The carbon-14 content is measured in percent modern carbon, or pMC. First, one measures the ratio of C-14 to the total carbon present in the coal, mostly carbon-12. Then this ratio is expressed as a percentage of the same C-14/C-12 ratio existing in the present-day atmosphere. The amounts of C-14 in coal are found to average 0.25 percent of that in the atmosphere today.

The carbon-14 data for coal in the table shows a ± uncertainty or error margin for each measurement. Most of the data in the other tables of this book also show ± values. This does not mean that the true value is necessarily sandwiched between these boundaries. For example, the first entry in Table 3-2 shows a carbon-14 content of 0.30 ± 0.03 pMC, which gives a range between 0.27 and 0.33. This is a statistical result and is equal to a total spread of two standard deviations. Standard deviation measures the variation of data from the mean or average. Standard deviation is often identified by the Greek letter sigma, σ. Thus the coal sample value is 0.30 ± 1σ pMC. Probability theory shows that if one were to make a large number of similar measurements, 68.3 percent of them would fall within ± 1σ of the center value. For the particular coal sample then, 68.3 percent of repeated measurements would fall

Table 3-2. The carbon-14 content for ten RATE samples of coal. The columns show the coal locations and their conventional geologic ages. The samples include Paleozoic, Mesozoic, and Cenozoic coals. The right column gives the quantity of measured carbon-14 in each sample in percent modern carbon, pMC, defined in the text. The laboratory subtracted a "background" of 0.08 pMC to obtain these values.

Coal Location and Geologic Era	Coal Seam	Conventional Geologic Age (Millions of Years)	C-14/C-12 (pMC ±1σ)
Cenozoic			
Texas	Bottom	34–55	0.30 ± 0.03
North Dakota	Beulah	34–55	0.20 ± 0.02
Montana	Pust	34–55	0.27 ± 0.02
Mesozoic			
Utah	Lower Sunnyside	65–145	0.35 ± 0.03
Utah	Blind Canyon	65–145	0.10 ± 0.03
Arizona	Green	65–145	0.18 ± 0.02
Paleozoic			
Kentucky	Kentucky #9	300–311	0.46 ± 0.03
Pennsylvania	Lykens Valley #2	300–311	0.13 ± 0.02
Pennsylvania	Pittsburgh	300–311	0.19 ± 0.02
Illinois	Illinois #6	300–311	0.29 ± 0.03
Average percent modern carbon for the ten coal samples is 0.247 ± 0.025			

between 0.27 and 0.33 pMC. This uncertainty in value is often due to the limits of the analytical chemistry and electronic equipment used in the measurement. It is important to keep this statistical definition in mind when radioisotope ages are given in future chapters. An alternate range of ± 2 σ is often used to describe uncertainty. This ± 2σ range gives a 95.4 percent chance of repeatability. For example, looking ahead to Table 6-1, which uses the ± 2σ convention, the entry for Grand Canyon sample MT-3 gives a conventional age of 535 ± 48 million

years. This does not imply the actual age of the rock must lie within the range 487–583 million years. Instead it means that, given a large group of equal-age, cogenetic samples, the ages measured in the laboratory will fall within this range 95.4 percent of the time, regardless of whether the calculated ages are right or wrong.

RATE CARBON-14 RESEARCH ON DIAMONDS

Diamonds are a crystalline form of pure carbon. They are thought to originate in the upper mantle at a depth of more than 150 kilometers (90 miles), where both pressure and temperature are extreme. At a later time, the diamonds may be carried to the earth's surface by upward-moving magma. There are indications that, in the past, some of this high-pressure, gas-charged magma surged upward at supersonic speeds of hundreds of miles per hour. This rising magma collected debris from the fractured rock strata it passed through as it burst upward and erupted at the surface. After cooling occurred, some of this hardened magma became a type of rock called *kimberlite* or *blue ground*. Another rock variety called *lamproite* may also crystallize from the cooling magma. The result is a long column called a *diamond pipe*. It spreads outward and becomes wider at the earth's surface, giving an underground shape somewhat like a giant carrot, hundreds of feet in diameter. During its formation, the pipe acts as a high-speed elevator, carrying dispersed diamonds to the surface. The diamonds are mined from these pipes in such locations as Australia, Brazil, Canada, Russia, and South Africa. Some of the largest excavations on earth are mined-out diamond pipes. Other pipes are tapped into from underground mines. Diamonds are also occasionally found in gravels called *placer* or *alluvial deposits*. These gems collect downstream from where kimberlite pipes once spewed out diamond-rich debris over the surrounding terrain.

The RATE team realized that natural diamonds would provide an extreme test of the pervasive presence of C-14 in earth materials.

Diamonds are typically assumed to be many millions of years old, if not billions. This vast age is based on the radioisotope dating of inclusions sometimes found inside diamonds. Diamond also is the hardest natural substance on earth. It therefore is very resistant to chemical alteration or contamination. The melting temperature of diamond is about 4,000°C, much higher than common metals. The carbon within diamond is assumed to have remained locked away from any exchange with the atmosphere since early in earth's history.

Twelve diamond samples were analyzed for possible carbon-14 content. These specimens originated from West and South Africa. They were about 0.25 carat in weight, or 50 milligrams each. The diamonds averaged two millimeters in diameter, about the thickness of two dimes. Unfortunately the AMS analysis for carbon-14 requires that the diamonds be destroyed. They are first crushed to very small chips, then rigorously and carefully cleaned, and finally burned, converting them to carbon dioxide. This gas is then condensed to a speck of graphite which the AMS instrument analyzes. In this process, one should not picture beautiful diamonds being hammered to dust! The raw, uncut diamonds analyzed by RATE have a rounded, glassy appearance. They are of industrial grade rather than gem quality, and are not excessively expensive.

The carbon-14 content measured for the 12 RATE diamonds is shown in Table 3-3. Similar to the earlier results for coal, all 12 diamond samples have detectable carbon-14 content, once again measured in percent modern carbon, pMC. The average C-14 content in the diamonds is 0.09 percent that of modern carbon, about one-third that found in coal. As far as we can determine, this RATE research marks the first time that carbon-14 measurements have been made on diamond. The presence of C-14 in "very old" fossils, rocks, coal, and diamond samples is clearly in major conflict with the long-age time scale.

Table 3-3. The carbon-14 content for 12 diamond samples from West and South Africa. The last seven diamond sources in the list are placer deposits found in stream beds. The right column gives the measured carbon-14 content in percent modern carbon, pMC, as defined in the text. The laboratory subtracted a "background" of 0.08 pMC to obtain these values.

Country of Origin	Diamond Location	C-14/C-12 (pMC ±1σ)
Botswana, South-Central Africa	Orapa mine	0.06 ± 0.03
	Orapa mine	0.03 ± 0.03
	Lethakane mine	0.04 ± 0.03
	Lethakane mine	0.07 ± 0.02
South Africa	Kimberley mine	0.02 ± 0.03
Guinea, West Africa	Kankan placer	0.03 ± 0.03
Namibia, Southwest Africa	Placer deposits	0.31 ± 0.02
(Six diamond samples)		0.17 ± 0.02
		0.09 ± 0.02
		0.13 ± 0.03
		0.04 ± 0.02
		0.07 ± 0.02
Average percent modern carbon for the 12 diamonds is 0.09 ± 0.025		

ATTEMPTS TO EXPLAIN TRACES OF C-14

Is there any way that new carbon-14 atoms could possibly enter and contaminate materials which are truly ancient? Three suggestions will be evaluated here. The first idea is that either the earth's atmosphere or moving groundwater somehow supplies old samples with new C-14 atoms. If true, this migration of carbon-14 would likely be an ongoing process throughout history. To maintain traces of radiocarbon in ancient material, the carbon content would have to be replaced many times over since carbon-14 is radioactive and does not last. The extreme variety in the thickness, depth, and porosity of the earth's rock layers would surely lead to great variation in C-14 contamination by air or water if this does indeed occur. However, the measured traces of C-14 are fairly uniform throughout the rock strata of the earth. Large-scale contamination of the earth's crustal rocks with carbon-14 from the environment is therefore not a reasonable explanation.

The second suggestion involves nuclear reactions in which outside neutrons enter samples and convert either nitrogen-14 or carbon-13 atoms directly to carbon-14. Such reactions can indeed occur, however, calculations show that the resulting C-14 amounts are several thousand times less than the range actually measured.

The third suggestion concerns heavy radioactive isotopes which exist in trace amounts in some samples. These include radium, thorium, and uranium atoms which can decay in several possible ways. A very small fraction of these decays produces carbon-14 atoms. In the case of radium-223, for example, somewhat less than one out of a billion decays produces a carbon-14 nucleus instead of the usual alpha particle. In this and every other case of radioactive decay, the C-14 production remains far below the amounts observed in diamonds. In fact, the generation of carbon-14 by the decay of heavy nuclei results in an amount at least 100,000 times less than the actual C-14 found in samples.

None of the three suggestions can sustain an ancient age while adequately explaining the presence of carbon-14 throughout the earth's crust. The conclusion is that the pervasive presence of C-14 is strong evidence for a youthful earth.

INTERPRETATION OF THE CARBON-14 DATA

How might the carbon-14 findings fit the young-earth view? One intriguing possibility involves the rock strata laid down by the global flood of Noah's day. During the pre-Flood centuries, the C-14 component of carbon was distributed uniformly throughout the earth's vegetation. This *biomass* then was rapidly buried and fossilized during the Flood which occurred about 4,500 years ago. The worldwide burial would lead to the fairly uniform traces of carbon-14 which are found throughout the earth's strata, no matter what depth of rock is tested. The entire Phanerozoic Eon encompassing the Paleozoic, Mesozoic, and Cenozoic Eras is considered by many creationists to be Flood-deposited rock.

The carbon-14 content of coal, diamonds, and many other earth materials varies between 0.1 and 0.5 percent modern carbon, pMC. These measured numbers translate into carbon-14 ages between 44,000 and 57,000 years based on several assumptions. Such ages are dramatically younger than their normally accepted ages, typically hundreds of millions of years. The RATE team concludes that a key assumption used in obtaining these carbon-14 ages is not correct because the ratio of carbon-14 to total carbon was almost certainly less during pre-Flood times than it is today. We know this from the great reservoir of fossil fuels which were buried during the Flood. This large biomass would have diluted the C-14 in the pre-Flood world to give a very low ratio of C-14/C-12 compared with the present world. The total amount of carbon found within carbonate rocks and fossil fuels, mostly carbon-12, is at least 100 times greater than that which resides in the total biosphere of living plants and animals today. Taking this pre-Flood carbon distribution into account, the carbon-14 ages for coal and diamonds is reduced to just several thousand years.

Another factor is that a stronger geomagnetic field existed during pre-Flood history than exists at present. This early earth magnetism would deflect cosmic rays away from the earth more efficiently than today and would diminish the historical production of carbon-14. Together, these factors can easily decrease the calculated carbon-14 dates of coal and diamond samples tenfold, from 50,000 to just 5,000 years, a value consistent with Flood history. The carbon-14 results from fossil materials cannot pin down biblical dates more precisely, because of the uncertainty in the actual amount of C-14 existing in the pre-Flood world.

There is another complementary creationist explanation for the presence of carbon-14 in earth materials. Some of the measured C-14 may be *primordial*, having been present in the earth from the beginning of time. In the young-earth view, the creation took place just a few thousand years ago. With the passing of time since creation equal to about one C-14 half-life, or 5,730 years, a measurable component of original C-14 would still remain.

ACCELERATED NUCLEAR DECAY

There is one final possible explanation for the carbon-14 residue found in earth materials. It was shown earlier in this chapter that the decay of heavy isotopes is incapable of producing the observed amounts of carbon-14, but this is only true at today's rates of disintegration. If nuclear decay was greatly accelerated in the past then substantial carbon-14 might have formed as a result. Alpha particles produced by uranium decay, for example, can interact with common elements in rocks such as oxygen, silicon, aluminum, and magnesium. As a result, neutrons are produced. These neutrons, in turn, can interact with underground nitrogen-14 and carbon-13 atoms to produce carbon-14. This could occur in both organic and mineral samples. The unexpected carbon-14 findings may be an indication of accelerated decay events in the past. The RATE team defines accelerated decay as millions of years' worth of nuclear decay, at present rates, taking place very quickly, perhaps in just days. Another way of describing accelerated decay is a temporary, extreme reduction in nuclear half-lives.

The carbon-14 content of the placer diamonds shows considerable variation (Table 3-3). One placer sample in particular has a percent modern carbon value of 0.31, higher than the other diamond samples measured. This suggests that some placer diamonds may have experienced intense nuclear reactions which produced their internal carbon-14 atoms. Perhaps the geological setting of these surface diamonds may have exposed them to the full effects of accelerated nuclear decay.

Since radiocarbon is still measured in samples today, the carbon-14 itself obviously did not completely decay away in the proposed acceleration process. The sped-up decay may well have depended on the particular half-lives involved. For example, suppose that all isotopes experienced a rapid 8 percent decay. Then uranium-238 with a 4.47 billion year half-life would undergo 540 million years of decay. An 8 percent decay of carbon-14 with its much shorter half-life of 5,730 years corresponds to only 690 years. Thus, there would remain a component of carbon-14 in samples which we still measure today. Accelerated nuclear decay certainly was more complicated than this example, and the concept will be further explored in the following chapters.

The RATE scientists are convinced that the popular idea attributed to geologist Charles Lyell from nearly two centuries ago, "The present is the key to the past," is simply not valid for an earth history of millions or billions of years. An alternative interpretation of the carbon-14 data is that the earth experienced a global flood catastrophe which laid down most of the rock strata and fossils. Also, many rates of change were accelerated in the recent past including sedimentary rock formation, erosion rates, and radioactive decay. Whatever the source of the carbon-14, its presence in nearly every sample tested worldwide is a strong challenge to an ancient age. Carbon-14 data is now firmly on the side of the young-earth view of history.

FURTHER STUDY

There is another radioactive isotope similar to carbon-14 which might provide valuable insight on the earth's age. This isotope is beryllium-10, Be-10, with a half-life of 1.52 million years. Somewhat similar to carbon-14, it results when cosmic rays collide with nitrogen and oxygen atoms in the earth's upper atmosphere. Fragmentation or *spallation* of the oxygen and nitrogen results in the formation of light-weight atoms including lithium, beryllium, and boron. This transformation also occurs on the outside surface of minerals which lie exposed on the ground. A technique called *cosmogenic exposure dating* is used to date these minerals. The concentration of beryllium-10 is taken as a measure of their total exposure time.

In deeply buried rocks, assumed to be ancient, any originally accumulated beryllium-10 atoms should be depleted by nuclear decay. However, there is mention in the geologic literature of Be-10 detected in these deep rocks (Faure and Mensing, 2005). This unexpected presence of Be-10 is very similar to the discovery of carbon-14 in samples. A worthwhile research program would entail the search for beryllium-10 in buried rock samples, perhaps obtained from drill cores. Any existing Be-10 from these lower levels would give additional evidence that the rocks, and the earth itself, are much younger than the standard geologic time scale implies.

Chapter 4

HELIUM RETENTION IN ZIRCON CRYSTALS

Research by Russell Humphreys

A Surprising Find

The previous chapter described unexpected carbon-14 atoms which are found in many "ancient" earth materials. This chapter highlights a similar situation of helium atoms residing where they should no longer exist. This helium is found deep underground within granite. Some of this "basement" rock was brought to the surface in 1974 during a deep-drilling project. The drilling was conducted at Fenton Hill, New Mexico, by geoscientists from the nearby Los Alamos National Laboratory (Figure 4-1). Holes were bored through solid rock to a depth of 4.3 kilometers or 2.6 miles. At this level, the temperature reaches 313°C (595°F) — well above the boiling point of water at the earth's surface. The purpose of the project was to explore whether underground heat could be tapped as a source of geothermal energy. The rock type retrieved from the boreholes is known as *granodiorite*, a common light-colored variety of granite with visible mineral crystals. The adjacent volcanic structure is known as the

Figure 4-1. The drilling rig used during the 1974 borehole project which sampled New Mexico basement rock. This drill reached a depth of 4.3 kilometers, or 2.6 miles. The photo is courtesy of Los Alamos National Laboratory.

Valles Caldera. It represents the collapsed central region of a massive volcano that erupted during the time of the Ice Age. The Los Alamos research team recorded the underground temperatures as they drilled and retrieved the rock samples. These samples were analyzed for their mineral and element composition. One component measured was the helium content of the minerals within the samples, and the results were astonishingly high. The significance of this result for creation studies begins with a description of zircon crystals.

RADIOACTIVE ZIRCON CRYSTALS

The main mineral components of granite rock include quartz, feldspar, and biotite. They can be seen as individual crystals that are usually millimeters in size. Quartz crystals have a cloudy-white or glassy color, while the feldspar is a shade of light gray or pink. Biotite crystals, also called *black mica*, occur in the granite as dark flakes. It typically comprises one to five percent of the granite. Within the biotite crystals themselves there often occur yet smaller crystals of zirconium silicate, the chief ore mineral of the metal zirconium. The name "zirconium" comes from an Arabic word meaning "golden color." The small crystals are called *zircons* and have the chemical formula $ZrSiO_4$.

The word *zircon* may be familiar to readers as the popular low-budget substitute for diamonds. However, the jewelry material is most often cubic zirconia with the chemical formula ZrO_2. Zirconia is made by chemical processes and does not form naturally. Actual zircon crystals are naturally occurring and are often smaller than a grain of sand. These small zircon crystals are found many places besides granite, including beach sand and even inside lunar rocks. Many zircon crystals are a few microns in size, a unit of length which is one-millionth of a meter. The thickness of a page of this book is about 100 microns. Larger zircons, centimeter size, also occur rarely and are prized as gemstones. In fact, zircon is listed as a December birthstone.

Large zircon crystals have been known since biblical times. They are identified in Old Testament texts with the terms *hyacinth* and *jacinth*. Figure 4-2 shows an optical microscope photograph of several small natural zircon crystals. Figure 4-3 is a scanning electron microscope picture of a single zircon crystal, enlarged about 1,300 times.

Granodiorite rock, present at the New Mexico drilling site, formed when molten magma cooled and crystallized underground. Zircons also grew during this process. As crystal growth proceeded, the zircons incorporated concentrations of radioactive uranium and thorium atoms. This occurred because these elements are chemically similar to the element zirconium. Up to four percent of the zirconium atoms in a crystal may be replaced by uranium and thorium. Figure 4-4 illustrates a fragment of granite with its component minerals.

Uranium-238, by far the most abundant isotope of uranium, decays to lead-206 through a series of steps during which eight alpha particles are released (Figure 4-5 and Table 4-1). Inside the larger zircons, 50 to 75 microns in size, many of the alpha particles remain. There they combine with nearby electrons to become helium atoms. The helium atoms are chemically inert, that is, they do not combine with other atoms to form molecules. They also are relatively small and remain in constant motion as gas particles. As a result, the helium is difficult to confine and behaves as a "slippery" material.

The New Mexico borehole rock is considered to be very old, about 1.5 billion years, based on lead-lead dating. It is classified as Precambrian which corresponds to the earliest part of the geologic time scale (Table 3-1). Within the zircon crystals, any helium atoms generated by nuclear decay in the distant past should have long ago migrated outward and escaped from these crystals. One would expect the helium gas to eventually diffuse upward out of the ground and then disappear into the atmosphere. To everyone's surprise, however, large amounts of helium have been found trapped inside the zircons. Much of it appears to have gone nowhere. For example, zircon from a

Figure 4-2. (Right) Optical microscope photograph of several zircon crystals. The crystal lengths are about 50 microns, or 0.002 inches, the size of small grains of sand. The photo is courtesy of Robert Gentry.

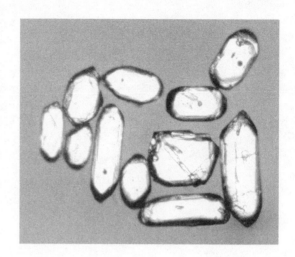

Figure 4-3. (Left) A scanning electron microscope photograph of a single zircon crystal, courtesy of Mark Armitage. The crystal is 75 microns in length, about the thickness of a page of this book. The zircon came from the New Mexico bore hole at a depth of 1,490 meters.

Granite

Granite close-up

Dark minerals are biotite

Figure 4-4. Diagram showing the major mineral components of granite. Tiny zircon crystals often are embedded in the mineral biotite. Many of these crystals in turn contain concentrations of uranium-238 atoms.

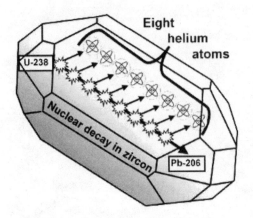

Figure 4-5. Illustration of a zircon crystal with its interior uranium, lead, and helium atoms. Eight helium atoms result from the complete decay of each radioactive uranium-238 atom to lead-206. See Table 4-1 for the details of U-238 decay.

Table 4-1. The decay of radioactive uranium-238 to stable lead-206 occurs in 14 steps. The downward arrows show the decay of each radioactive atom to the next step in the chain. During the entire decay process eight alpha (α) and six beta (β) particles are released. Most of these decays also emit gamma radiation. There is some variation in the reported isotope half-lives.

Isotope	Type of Radiation Emitted		Half-life
↓ Uranium-238	α (1st)		4.47 billion years
↓ Thorium-234		β (1st)	24 days
↓ Protactinium-234		β (2nd)	6.7 hours
↓ Uranium-234	α (2nd)		240,000 years
↓ Thorium-230	α (3rd)		77,000 years
↓ Radium-226	α (4th)		1602 years
↓ Radon-222	α (5th)		3.8 days
↓ Polonium-218	α (6th)		3.1 minutes
↓ Lead-214		β (3rd)	27 minutes
↓ Bismuth-214		β (4th)	20 minutes
↓ Polonium-214	α (7th)		0.000164 seconds
↓ Lead-210		β (5th)	22 years
↓ Bismuth-210		β (6th)	5 days
↓ Polonium-210	α (8th)		138 days
Lead-206			stable

depth of 1,000 meters was found to hold 58 percent of the total helium generated by past nuclear decay, and most of the 42 percent that left the zircon appears to have gone no farther than into the surrounding biotite mineral. Zircon samples from 2,900 meters deep retain 17 percent of their total helium. One expects this decrease in helium content with greater depth because the temperature is higher. This heat speeds up the overall movement of atoms and the diffusion of helium out of the zircon crystals. However, for both depths the large amounts of resident helium were totally unexpected. The initial helium measurements were made by creation scientist Robert Gentry in 1982 while he worked at Oak Ridge National Laboratory in Tennessee. The results are reported in the geoscience literature.

There is obviously something wrong, either with the assumed time scale of the New Mexico rock formation, or else with the understanding of helium movement through rock. Aware of these data, the RATE team formed a significant hypothesis: the large amount of helium existing in zircons might be the result of an episode of accelerated nuclear decay that occurred just thousands of years ago. Then, because the helium was formed recently, much of it still remains inside the zircon crystals, having had insufficient time to leak out. The RATE team concluded that helium in zircons provided an important creation research opportunity.

RATE RESEARCH ON HELIUM DIFFUSION

An initial suggestion was that the biotite mineral surrounding the zircon crystals might act as a barrier to keep the helium atoms trapped inside the embedded crystals indefinitely. To evaluate this idea, the RATE team needed to know the ease with which helium atoms migrate through both the biotite and the zircon crystals. A literature search yielded only sketchy information on helium diffusion in zircons, and no information at all on helium diffusion in biotite. Such measurements simply had not been reported by anyone in the literature. Diffusion experiments in minerals require experience, specific equipment, and very precise control of conditions. The RATE scientists, therefore, through an intermediary, commissioned the help and expertise of one of the world's foremost experts in helium diffusion measurements.

Flakes of biotite were prepared for the initial helium diffusion studies. The mineral was separated from a rock sample previously collected in Wyoming near Yellowstone National Park. This sample was from the Beartooth Mountains area and was a metamorphic variety called amphibolite. The results showed a relatively high rate of diffusion of helium in biotite. That is, the helium atoms were found to move quite easily through the biotite mineral crystal structure. Theoretical RATE studies also showed that the interface or contact surface between the biotite and zircon minerals should not be a barrier or hindrance to the movement of helium atoms. The helium atoms should readily diffuse out of the zircon crystals over geologic time.

Encouraged by the initial biotite diffusion results, several rock samples were obtained by request from the 1974 Los Alamos borehole project. They were taken from a depth of 750 meters, where the temperature was measured at a constant 96°C, just below the boiling point of water. A sample was sent to Activation Laboratories in Ontario, Canada, where the biotite and zircon components were separated. The zircons were dated using the uranium-lead method. The age was determined as 1,439 ± 2 million years, in close agreement with the previous 1.5 billion year age reported 20 years earlier.

Next, diffusion data were obtained for the biotite and the zircons. The procedure included heating the minerals to various temperatures in steps of about 25°C and carefully measuring the rate at which helium atoms were "baked" out and released. Each temperature step required a full hour of helium counting. Helium diffusion in the biotite mineral was found to be about ten times greater than in zircons. This further confirmed that it was the zircon crystals themselves which held onto the helium with little interference from the surrounding biotite.

Additional rock samples were obtained from a depth of 1,490 meters, where the temperature is 124°C. Many hundreds of zircon crystals were separated from these samples and sorted by crystal size. As one can imagine, the process of freeing the tiny zircon crystals from hard rock and then comparing their sizes was a slow and tedious process. The larger crystals, typically 50–75 microns long and half as wide were selected for additional diffusion measurements. Some 1,200 of these crystals were sent to the diffusion laboratory. Their total combined mass was only 0.35 milligrams, less than that of a single staple. Valuable helium diffusion data was gathered from these zircons.

RESULTS OF HELIUM DIFFUSION IN ZIRCON

The results for the helium diffusion experiments are shown in Figure 4-6 along with other information. First, consider the two quantities which are plotted. The horizontal axis of the graph shows temperature increasing from left to right. This is the reverse of the standard way that diffusion graphs are usually constructed. The temperature is measured in degrees centigrade. The uppermost black circle on the right shows the increased helium diffusion in zircon at a temperature of 550°C or 1,022°F. The lowermost black circle shows helium diffusion at 171°C, or 340°F.

The vertical axis records the diffusion coefficient or diffusivity with units of centimeters^2/second. This quantity measures the ease with which helium atoms leave the zircon crystals. The numbers show that the vertical axis is logarithmic in nature. That is, this axis telescopes together a great range of diffusion values covering 12 decimal places, from 10^{-23} to 10^{-11}, a trillion-fold variation in diffusion ability. The

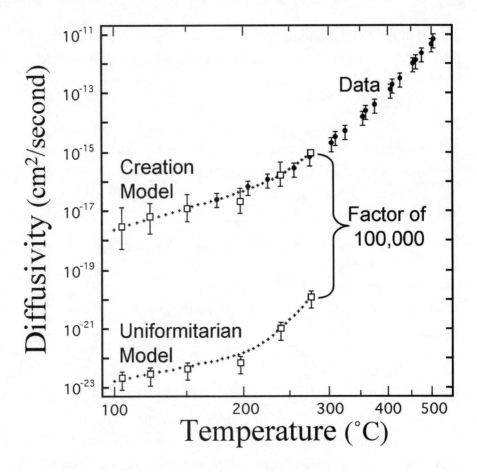

Figure 4-6. A summary of data for the escape of helium atoms from zircon crystals. Diffusivity is plotted against temperature. The solid black dots show the measured data. Also shown are the calculated predictions for helium diffusion according to creation (upper squares) and conventional long-age (lower squares) models. The error bars show ± 2 standard deviation bounds on the data and models. Further graph details are explained in the text.

diffusion of atoms through matter is one of the few properties of nature which have this wide a range of possible values.

The black circles on the graph show the actual RATE measurements of helium diffusion in zircons at different temperatures.

THOUSANDS . . . NOT BILLIONS

As one would expect, higher temperatures increase the diffusion ability of the helium atoms. As a result, the data points swing upward to the right. To understand the squares shown in Figure 4-6, we need to consider another useful item of data related to diffusion. This is the actual amount of helium present within the zircons and the surrounding biotite. Robert Gentry obtained some of this information during his early studies. Additional new data were collected by the RATE group for the New Mexico samples taken from a depth of 1,490 meters. The helium amounts were measured in the same laboratory where the diffusion experiments were carried out. A helium concentration was found for the biotite mineral averaging 6.6 nanomoles/cm^3. For the zircon, the helium concentration is about 200 times greater, 1,320 nanomoles/cm^3. A nanomole of helium is a billionth of a mole, or 6.02×10^{14} atoms. This is a large number; however, the other atoms making up the biotite material typically number a billion times greater. This means that the helium atoms in the biotite and zircons represent only a very small impurity.

Now let us return to the squares shown in Figure 4-6. Knowing the amount of helium present in the zircons, and assuming a given time scale, the expected value of diffusivity can be calculated for different temperatures. This requires detailed theoretical calculations which also were part of the RATE research. *Mathematica* software was utilized for the solution of the equations. In essence, the software divides the amount of helium lost at each temperature by the time during which it was lost. This time was either 6,000 years or 1.5 billion years depending on the model used. The lower level squares represent the predicted diffusion for the conventional long-age model. A very small helium diffusion value is required because the zircons are assumed to be 1.5 billion years old, yet they still possess considerable helium. In contrast, the young-earth model assumes a much shorter history for the zircons. The upper squares show the calculated helium diffusion based on a time scale of just 6,000 years. Note the close fit between the experimental diffusion data (black circles) and the creation model (upper squares).

The difference in calculated helium diffusion values between the two models is very large as indicated by the logarithmic numbers on the vertical scale. The long-age evolution model requires diffusion to be 100,000 times slower than is actually measured. Actually, the conflict which arises with deep time is even more serious than shown by Figure 4-6. The black data points are based on the retained helium in zircons which were taken from an underground depth where the temperature is currently 124°C. However, geologists believe that this rock has experienced several pulses of higher temperatures in the distant past due to the movement of magma in the region. They estimate increases in underground rock temperature between 50°C and 200°C, lasting for thousands to millions of years. If true, this added heat would greatly increase diffusion in past history and should quickly empty the zircons of most of their helium content. The RATE team rejects the long-age scale of these heat pulses, but the implication is clear: The conventional model requires that helium diffusion be even less than that shown by the lower squares in Figure 4-6. Therefore, the conflict with deep time is even greater than the 100,000 factor shown.

Based on the measured helium retention, statistical analysis gives an estimated age for the zircons of 6,000 ± 2,000 years. This age agrees with literal biblical history and is about 250,000 times shorter than the conventional age of 1.5 billion years for the zircons. The conclusion is that helium diffusion data strongly supports the young-earth view of history.

CLOSURE TEMPERATURE

Some skeptics of the helium diffusion results have brought up the concept of closure temperature. The argument is that below a certain temperature, called *closure*, helium atoms do not have sufficient energy to escape the zircons. The suggestion is that the helium will be held captive even for billions of years. However, the closure definition does not mean that helium migration out of the zircon crystal is eliminated. Instead, closure is defined as the temperature, as rock cools, below which the formation of helium by uranium decay will begin to exceed the loss of helium by diffusion. As the helium content builds up, however, the diffusion will increase accordingly. Eventually, on a long time scale, the zircon must lose helium as fast as nuclear decay produces it. The diffusion researcher commissioned by RATE calculated a closure temperature for zircon of about 128°C. The basic mechanism of diffusion does not change at this temperature and the measurements shown in Figure 4-6 apply just as certainly below 128°C as above. The bottom line is that closure temperature does not seal zircon crystals to helium loss and does not explain the measured helium retention in these crystals.

FURTHER DISCUSSION OF ZIRCONS

One critic of the RATE project asserted a novel explanation as to why abundant helium atoms exist in zircons. The proposal involves the biotite mineral which surrounds the zircon crystals. Biotite is a form of mica which forms in thin, flat layers. The suggestion was that the biotite layers wrapped tightly around the zircons like multiple layers of cellophane. The zircons were hermetically sealed with no possible way for the helium atoms to ever escape. However, microscope observations do not show the biotite layers wrapping around the edges of zircon crystals and sealing them as proposed. Instead, the zircon crystals are simply sandwiched between the flat mica layers. The evidence does not support the suggestion of sealed-up zircons.

The retention of helium atoms in the biotite flakes was earlier shown to be about 200 times less than that in the embedded zircon crystals. The high helium concentration in the zircons assures that helium will naturally move outward instead of the reverse. The laws of diffusion require any concentration of free atoms to spread outward and dissipate. The comparison of biotite and zircon retention shows that it is the zircons themselves which restrain the helium atoms, not the outside biotite material. As expected, the total helium measured in the much larger biotite flakes is roughly equal to the amount which has been lost by the tiny embedded zircons.

Zircon crystals are thought to be some of the oldest minerals on earth (Mathez, 2004). They are very hard and resistant to deterioration, and therefore are thought to preserve their contents over extremely long periods of time. Zircon crystals from Canadian gneiss (pronounced *nīce*) rock have been dated at over 4 billion years old, and zircons found in Australia are said to be 4.4 billion years old. The RATE research does not challenge, but rather affirms the existence of billions of years' worth of the daughter products of uranium decay in these zircons. But RATE also finds in the zircons a large fraction of the helium generated by this same uranium decay. The RATE helium diffusion measurements show that such high concentrations of helium simply cannot be sustained for more than a few thousand years. The only way we can reconcile the observed amount of uranium decay with the observed levels of helium retention is with one or more periods of accelerated nuclear decay in the earth's recent past. We conclude that the RATE helium diffusion experiments give strong evidence for accelerated decay of the uranium atoms inside zircon crystals, and a young age for the earth.

Chapter 5

RADIOHALOS IN GRANITE

Research by Andrew Snelling

FINGERPRINTS FROM RADIATION

The atoms within most solids, including rocks and minerals, are lined up in orderly arrays of rows, columns, and layers. Figure 5-1 shows the crystal lattice arrangement for a zircon crystal, $ZrSiO_4$. A sand grain-size crystal actually contains trillions of atoms in a repeated pattern. This remarkable three-dimensional architecture is based on the chemical bonding between atoms and gives rise to the distinct flat outside surfaces of crystals. As explained in chapter 4, zircons may contain noteworthy concentrations of radioactive elements.

When the decay of a radioactive atom such as uranium takes place inside a solid crystalline material, a permanent record may be left behind in the form of microscopic tracks of damage. The electrically

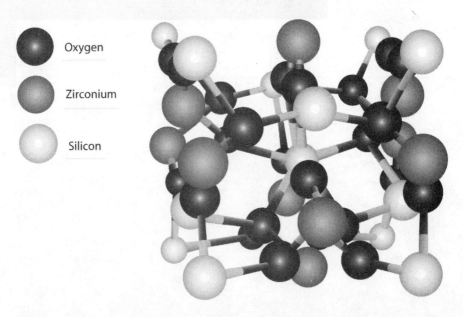

Oxygen

Zirconium

Silicon

Figure 5-1. An illustration of the ordered arrangement of atoms in a crystal. Shown is the structure for zircon, $ZrSiO_4$. The dark spheres represent oxygen atoms. The shaded and light spheres are divided between zirconium and silicon atoms.

charged particles emitted during nuclear decay, especially alpha particles, can disrupt the nearby atomic arrangement. That is, the atoms and electrons may be displaced from their normal positions. Widespread radiation damage from many alpha particles can even produce a visible darkening of the entire crystal.

Examples of radiation damage in crystals include radioactive halos, or radiohalos. Because of the dark color of these crystal defects they are also called *pleochroic halos*. They are fascinating examples of radiation effects or "burns" in crystals. Microscopic halos were first noted over a century ago, and their connection with radiation was proposed by Irish geologist John Joly in 1907.

The formation of a radiohalo requires a concentration of radioactivity called a *radiocenter*. This often occurs within igneous rocks as they solidify from molten magma. Radioactive uranium and thorium atoms tend to cluster within the mineral called *zircon*, $ZrSiO_4$. Zircon crystals were introduced in the previous chapter as reservoirs for radioactive uranium and helium atoms. The tiny zircon crystal as a whole becomes a radiocenter. Over time, the radioactive atoms within a grain of zircon will experience decay, sending alpha particles outward randomly in all directions. Larger zircon crystals, those 50 or more microns or millionths of a meter in length, tend to trap many of the alphas which become helium atoms. This helium was the topic of the previous chapter. Other zircon crystals are much smaller, less than a single micron in diameter. Many alpha particles will exit such crystals and pass into the surrounding biotite mineral. The alpha particles gradually lose their kinetic energy, slow down, and stop. Most of the interaction with the biotite occurs toward the end of their path. All the alpha particles with a particular initial energy stop at roughly the same distance away from the radiocenter. The result is a thin spherical shell of discoloration surrounding the zircon. A large number of alpha particles are required to form a visible radiohalo, typically on the order of 500 million. This amounts to about 100 million years of decay of an isotope such as uranium-238, at present rates. The existence of radiohalos is clear evidence that much nuclear decay has occurred. However, biblical and scientific evidence greatly limits the time scale. As we shall see, the RATE team sees the existence of certain radiohalos as evidence for accelerated nuclear decay.

The radiohalo spheres are typically 10-40 microns in diameter. Figure 5-2 illustrates the starburst pattern of alpha particles moving outward from the radiocenter. Multiple rings often occur, made by alpha particles with distinct energies. The alpha particles with greater energy travel farther and produce the larger rings (Figure 5-3).

Although radiohalos are actually spherical in shape, when viewed in cross section they appear as concentric rings. The halos typically occur in biotite, a mineral that easily breaks apart into thin sheets called

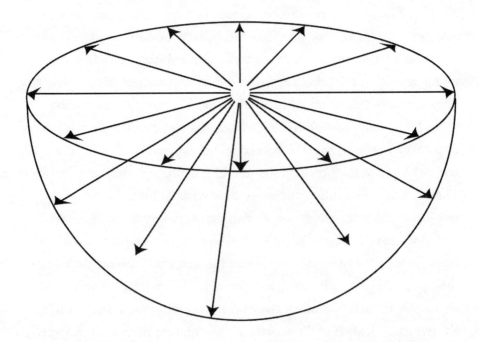

Figure 5-2. An illustration of the starburst pattern of alpha particles leaving a radiocenter and forming a radiohalo. Alpha particles with higher energy form shells with a larger radius.

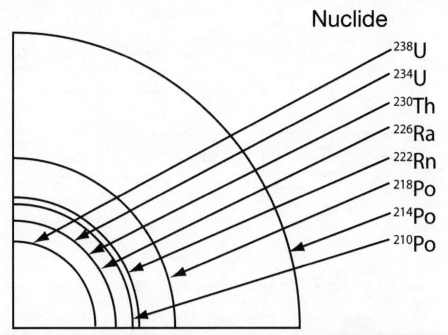

Figure 5-3. The drawing shows a one-quarter section of the circular halos resulting from the decay of uranium-238. The rings are formed by alpha particles emitted during nuclear decay. The radii are proportional to the alpha energies. For U-238 there are eight distinct rings, some overlapping. They correspond to the eight alpha particles listed in Table 4-1.

cleavage planes. Perhaps you have seen sheets of mica, also called *isinglass* in days gone by. In its translucent form called *muscovite,* mica once served as window panes. Biotite is just one of several types of mica. If a biotite sample contains radiohalos, its sheets can be peeled away to reveal a slice that cuts through these halos and shows circular sets of rings. The largest ring is found when the radiocenter is visible, which represents the maximum size of the radiohalo (Figure 5-4). The process is similar to slicing an onion horizontally to reveal its internal layers that appear as rings.

Radiohalos can form only within a solid crystalline structure since they are a record of defects or damage to the alignment of atoms. If radiohalos are observed in an igneous rock formation, they must have

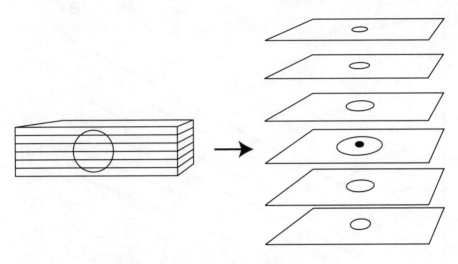

Figure 5-4. Illustration of a spherical radiohalo intersecting many layers within the mineral biotite. The layers are peeled (right side of the figure) to obtain the center layer. This is the circle with maximum size and the zircon radiocenter (black dot).

formed after the rock cooled and solidified. In addition, if the rock is reheated at a later time, the radiohalos will fade and disappear as the crystal atoms realign themselves and repair the crystal defects. The temperature where this occurs is called the *annealing* temperature, about 150°C (302°F) for the mineral biotite. Therefore, the presence of radiohalos provides useful information on the temperature history of rocks.

Details of the radioactive decay of uranium and thorium atoms are well known. Uranium-238 decays to the stable lead-206 isotope in several steps, as shown in Table 4-1. During the entire process, eight alpha particles with distinct energies are released. Figure 5-3 shows the rings or halos that result from the decay of uranium-238. Thorium-232 likewise releases six alphas during its decay to lead-208. The measurement of the diameters of these rings provides information on the alpha particle energies. This in turn identifies the radioactive isotopes present in the zircon crystals, much like a fingerprint identifies an individual.

A Radiohalo Mystery

There is an intriguing mystery involving radiohalos. It concerns those halos which result from the decay of three particular isotopes of the element polonium:

Isotope	Half-life
Po-210	138 days
Po-214	0.000164 seconds
Po-218	3.1 minutes

Each of these radioactive isotopes gives off an alpha particle upon its decay. Note that these polonium isotopes have relatively brief half-lives. They are short-lived and all three result from steps late in the decay of uranium-238 (Table 4-1). The decay of a sufficient number of polonium atoms within a crystal will produce a radiohalo. However, the observed polonium halos often show no evidence whatsoever of rings resulting from the other decay steps as the uranium-238 transforms to lead. Since the uranium-238 decay chain produces eight alpha particles, finding halos with three or fewer rings implies at least five rings are missing. The mystery is how the short-lived polonium atoms come to be embedded in crystalline rock without uranium atoms existing at the same location. How do these "parentless" or "orphan" halos originate? It is almost as if the polonium atoms suddenly appear within the solid rock and then decay. One possible interpretation is that the polonium atoms were instantly placed within granite at the moment of creation, at which time they quickly decayed and formed permanent radiohalos. In this case, the halos would be evidence for an instant supernatural creation of the original rock foundations of the earth. The RATE studies show that this interpretation of polonium radiohalos is not correct; their origin is a bit more complicated.

RATE Radiohalo Research

Radiohalos are important for RATE investigation since these crystal features provide visible information on the history of nuclear decay. Two questions may be addressed. First, do the parentless polonium radiohalos actually provide evidence for an instantaneous, supernatural creation or is there another explanation for their existence? The second question involves the actual distribution of radiohalos throughout the rocks of the earth. A natural dividing point is the global flood of Noah's day. How then do the numbers of radiohalos compare for pre-Flood, Flood, and post-Flood rocks?

The RATE studies included a survey of the geologic distribution of radiohalos. Three distinct groups of igneous rocks were collected, all granites. The first group consisted of rocks categorized by geologists as Precambrian, the oldest rocks on earth (Table 3-1). In the creation view, such rock formations date from pre-Flood history and some quite likely are remnants of the original created earth. The distinction is less clear between rocks dating from the creation week and those formed up to the time of the Flood.

Group two consists of granites associated with Paleozoic-Mesozoic sedimentary rock strata that formed more recently than Precambrian. These rocks often contain fossils, implying they are Flood deposits. The RATE granite samples result from molten magma which flowed underground, cooled, and hardened. Much of this igneous material is intruded directly into the fossil-bearing rock layers deposited during the Flood event. An approximate date for these rocks and for the Flood itself is 4,500 years ago.

The final group of rocks surveyed by the RATE team is from the latter Cenozoic era and is most likely late-Flood and post-Flood in age with a fairly recent formation. In summary, here is a broad generalization of rock strata:

Youngest	Cenozoic Era	Late- and post-Flood deposits
	Mesozoic Era	Mid- and late-Flood deposits
	Paleozoic Era	Early-Flood deposits
Oldest	Precambrian Era	Creation week and pre-Flood deposits

The exact pre-Flood, early, middle, and post-Flood boundaries are still under investigation, but the geologic eras provide a broad, useful outline.

The examination of granite rocks for radiohalos is an involved process. Initially, the rocks were collected with careful documentation of their location, often from remote areas. Efforts were made to obtain freshly exposed samples. Back in the laboratory, flakes of biotite about a millimeter in size were pried loose from the sample. In some cases, the hard granite rock was crushed to retrieve the biotite. The flakes then were hand-picked and placed between layers of clear adhesive tape. The thin layers of biotite were separated by peeling the tape apart. This peeling process was repeated until very thin transparent flakes of biotite remained, and they were mounted on a microscope slide. Approximately 20–30 flakes were placed on one slide, and 50 slides were prepared for each RATE sample. A single granite rock sample thus yielded a minimum of 1,000 biotite flakes for observation. Each flake was examined with a microscope. Figure 5-5 shows photomicrographs of polonium radiohalos in the mineral biotite.

With over one hundred granite samples studied altogether, well over 5,000 slides were prepared and examined in the RATE study, perhaps one of the largest radiohalo surveys ever conducted. All radiohalos observed in the biotite flakes were tabulated and the next section summarizes the results.

RADIOHALO COUNTS AND ANALYSIS

Table 5-1 gives the radiohalo results for all of the RATE granite samples. Starting with the oldest, there were a total of 1,510 glass slides

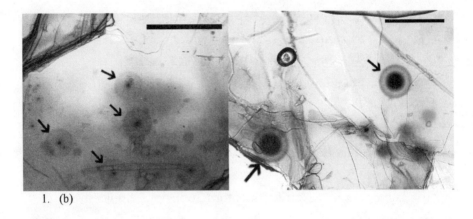

1. (b)

Figure 5-5. Photomicrograph of radiohalos (arrows) in the mineral biotite, courtesy of Mark H. Armitage. Polonium-210 halos are on the left and polonium-218 halos on the right. The black bars in the upper right corners are 60 microns long. The halos are about 0.02 millimeters in diameter, the size of dust grains.

prepared from 31 samples of Precambrian granite. These rocks were collected from many locations including Finland, Australia, and six western U.S. states. Some of the slides revealed no radiohalos while others showed many. The average count was 1.54 radiohalos per slide. The majority of the halos for all three groups were found to result from the decay of polonium-210 atoms. There was a relatively small number of radiohalos found in Precambrian rocks. This may result from the heating of these rocks during tectonic upheaval brought on by the Flood. Heating above the annealing temperature erases any existing radiohalos. Most, if not all, of the radiohalos found today in Precambrian rock probably were generated at a later time, perhaps during and after the Flood.

Table 5-1 also gives the radiohalo results for the granites dated as Paleozoic-Mesozoic in age (Table 3-1). There were 70 rocks sampled from Australia, England, Norway, and the United States. A total of 3,485 slides were prepared and examined. The average number

Table 5-1. Summary of the numbers of radiohalos found in granite rocks from the three geologic divisions Precambrian, Paleozoic-Mesozoic, and Tertiary. One creationist interpretation is that these divisions represent pre-Flood, Flood, and post-Flood rocks. The conventional ages are given in millions of years, or Ma. Also shown are radiohalo counts for metamorphic rocks. The observed halos are matched to the listed isotopes.

Conventional age of rock	Number of rock samples (Number of slides prepared)	Number of halos counted				
		Po-210	Po-214	Po-218	U-238	Th-232
Tertiary 1Ma-65Ma	8(400)	9	0	0	2	0
	Average number of radiohalos per slide = 0.028					
Paleozoic-Mesozoic 70Ma - 490Ma	70(3,485)	15,847	1,350	426	11,092	286
	Average = 8.32					
Precambrian 600Ma – 2,900Ma	31(1,510)	1,788	23	2	510	3
	Average = 1.54					
Metamorphic Rocks 100Ma-1,750Ma	21(1,051)	8,999	53	11	2,971	3
	Average = 11.45					

of halos per slide is 8.32, about five times higher than for the older Precambrian group of rocks. Since this second group of granites is directly Flood-related, an immediate conclusion is that not all radiohalos date from the creation week. Instead it appears that major radiohalo formation occurred during the year of the Genesis flood. Since the radiohalos result from radioactive decay, the conclusion then follows that nuclear decay was greatly accelerated during the Flood event.

Previous studies by Robert Gentry and others explored possible changes in the size of uranium radiohalos. The distance from the edges of the zircon radiocenters to their outer rings is found to be fairly constant. This indicates that the alpha particle energies have remained constant through history, even during episodes of accelerated decay. These decay episodes give rise to another problem which is the dissipation of immense amounts of heat when radioactive decay is accelerated. This heat problem is addressed in chapter 9.

The upper entries of Table 5-1 show the radiohalo results for the most recent granite rocks. Tertiary is one of the subdivisions of the Cenozoic era. Eight rock samples were collected from four western U.S. states and 400 slides were prepared. Only 11 halos were found, all appearing on two slides from a Washington granite sample. This is not surprising since there has been little time for radioactive decay since these rocks formed, and apparently little or no acceleration of decay activity has occurred during late-Flood and post-Flood history.

Figure 5-6 summarizes the radiohalo data from Table 5-1. The horizontal axis records the conventional geological age for rock samples. The vertical axis gives the number of radiohalos per slide for all of the samples. The figure shows that the great majority of observed radiohalos occur in rocks formed during the Flood event.

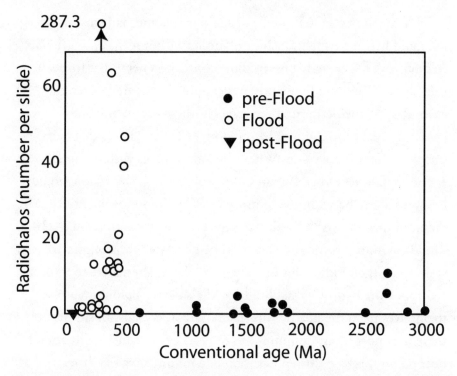

Figure 5-6. The graph summarizes measured radiohalo counts versus conventional geologic time in Ma (millions of years). The vertical axis gives the number of radiohalos per slide for the RATE granite samples. Notice that Flood rocks show the largest numbers of observed radiohalos. The data point far above the others, 287.3 radiohalos per slide, is for a granite sample from Cornwall, England.

PARENTLESS RADIOHALOS

What about the polonium halos which appear without any parent uranium atoms present? For several years there has been discussion and debate about the possible rapid movement of polonium atoms away from their uranium source within crystals. Perhaps they could be carried along by hydrothermal fluids which include hot water solutions and gases. The polonium could then be deposited elsewhere to form a secondary radiohalo at some distance from the primary uranium-238 source atoms.

RATE studies refined the details of possible mechanisms involving the rapid hydrothermal transport of atoms within rocks and minerals. Radiohalos are generally observed in biotite, a mineral that forms in thin sheets. There are frequently indications that heated water and gases at one time permeated the layers of these biotite minerals. One decay product of uranium-238 is radon-222 (Rn-222) with a half-life of 3.8 days (Table 4-1). When the radon forms within a small zircon crystal, it readily migrates outward as a gas. This radon would be swept along between the biotite planes by fluid movement. The radon in turn decays through the steps Po-218, Po-214, and Po-210. These polonium isotopes then would be deposited or precipitated at sites where their radiohalos quickly form. As an alternative to radium transport, the hydrothermal fluid could also carry polonium atoms themselves from the nearby "upstream" zircon crystals. In support of these transport ideas, uranium-238 radiohalos are consistently found near polonium halos, often less than one millimeter away. Their centers are usually in the same biotite layer. Also, polonium halos often are centered on small hollow bubbles in the biotite mineral, as if these were openings where the polonium isotopes collected. In contrast, the uranium halos are centered on zircon crystals. The polonium halos, similar to the uranium halos, are always located along cleavages, cracks, or crystal defects which would serve as conduits for fluid infiltration. The isotope transport activity would take place during the latter stages of crystallization and cooling of the granite magmas.

There is additional evidence for the fluid transport of atoms in biotite. Traces of sulfur are frequently found within the cleavages of biotite flakes. It is known that the element polonium has an attraction or affinity for sulfur and certain other elements. Sulfur atoms existing within the biotite thus may provide sites where the polonium isotopes collect or accumulate. There are similar reports from other geologic locations of isotope movement by hydrothermal fluids. Polonium-210 has been detected in volcanic gases and also in fluids ejected from deep sea vents. In some of these cases the polonium isotopes are estimated to have traveled several kilometers during the course of days or weeks. With the much shorter travel distance within biotite flakes, usually just microns or millimeters, the process of hydrothermal fluid transport may help solve the mystery of the parentless polonium radiohalos. The formation of secondary polonium halos by rapid fluid transport remains a tentative theory. More research is clearly needed on these intriguing halos. Yet geologists know that crustal fluids play a significant part in many underground processes, and this may well include the formation of the parentless polonium radiohalos.

Much of the hydrothermal fluid which transports and relocates the isotopes is generated as the magma crystallizes. The presence of the short-lived polonium halos indicates that the magma cooled to solid rock very rapidly rather than over long ages as often assumed. The circulating water would serve to carry away and dissipate heat from the magma body. The existence of so many polonium halos in the rocks of Flood age appears to require an extreme amount of accelerated nuclear decay during this period. There is a narrow window of time from when the temperature falls below the annealing temperature until the rocks cool so much that fluids can no longer penetrate the biotite crystal structure. The parentless polonium halos point to a young age for these rocks and for the earth exactly as Robert Gentry predicted years ago.

Radiohalos in Metamorphic Rocks

Metamorphic rocks form underground when existing rocks are altered by high temperature, pressure, hydrothermal fluids, or chemical changes. Melting also occurs in extreme metamorphism. These factors change the rock's appearance and crystal structure. For example, limestone converts to marble, and shale becomes slate. Extreme metamorphism progressively produces rocks such as schist, gneiss, and even granite where melting has occurred. Metamorphic rocks have experienced a high degree of heating, so all preexisting radiohalos would be erased by annealing. The presence of radiohalos in rocks such as gneiss requires the halo formation to occur after the rock cools below about 150°C. Parentless polonium radiohalos found in these altered rocks would be strong evidence for the hydrothermal fluid transport concept. Few metamorphic rocks, however, have ever been examined for radiohalo content. To address this overlooked area, the RATE radiohalo work included collection of 21 metamorphic rocks from Australia, Norway, and the Grand Canyon area. Radiohalos then were sought within the prepared samples. The lower entry of Table 5-1 lists the results. Polonium radiohalos were indeed found in the metamorphic rocks in large numbers similar to the granite rocks that were studied. This suggests that hydrothermal fluids circulated through the metamorphic materials during or after their cooling. As before, these fluids transported short-lived polonium isotopes through the rock to sites where they accumulated and then generated the observed radiohalos.

The possibility that hot fluid flow is commonplace in metamorphic rocks has far-reaching implications for the geologic understanding of metamorphism. Metamorphic rocks comprise a major portion of the earth's crust, and the full details of their origin have remained uncertain. Here we see that their formation from other rocks may well require circulating fluids. The largely ignored polonium radiohalos may thus give important insight into extremely important geological processes.

There is a potential economic application of polonium radiohalos. They appear to be associated with rapid hydrothermal fluid transport, a mechanism also responsible for the underground deposition of many metallic ore deposits. Metal ions such as copper, zinc, silver, tin, gold, lead, and uranium are commonly carried along in solution by hydrothermal fluids, and then later deposited. The presence of radiohalos in rocks might be a predictor that concentrations of some of these metals are located in the vicinity. Thus polonium radiohalos could be a valuable exploration tool in prospecting for metal ores.

Chapter 6

FISSION TRACKS IN ZIRCONS

Research by Andrew Snelling

FORMATION OF FISSION TRACKS

Similar to radiohalos, fission tracks represent another permanent record of nuclear decay within crystalline solids. They were first observed several decades ago during the microscopic examination of solids which had been exposed to radiation. The tracks result when a heavy, unstable atom spontaneously fissions or splits into two smaller atoms. These fission fragments then fly apart in opposite directions at high speed. Since they are themselves heavy and electrically charged, a single fragment can produce a significant track of damage in the crystal structure. Atoms within the surrounding crystal are pulled out of alignment and some of their electrons may be stripped away. The tracks appear mainly in electrical insulators where the electrons are not free to move about and return to their equilibrium position.

Tracks often are observed in glass and ceramics, and their occurrence is used by archaeologists to date such objects. The fission tracks or channels have a tubular shape and are typically 10–15 microns long. In minerals, the dominant source for fission tracks is the isotope uranium-238. One of the many ways that uranium may fission is to produce two palladium atoms:

$$U\text{-}238 \rightarrow Pd\text{-}119 + Pd\text{-}119$$

This spontaneous fission of U-238 rarely occurs at today's measured rates. For every two million uranium-238 atoms which undergo alpha decay, itself a slow process (Table 2-1), only a single U-238 atom undergoes decay by fission (Ohanian, 1985). Nevertheless, fission tracks are common in minerals and natural glass. As with radiohalos, the fission tracks disappear when a rock sample is heated above an annealing temperature. Various minerals lose their tracks at different temperatures. Fission tracks therefore provide information on the thermal history of samples. However, the annealing temperatures for various minerals, ranging between 50°–400°C, are not well known.

FISSION TRACK DATING

Dating of minerals by fission track counting is a widely used clock or geochronometer. An interior surface of a sample is exposed by a grinding process. This new surface is then polished smooth and etched with an acid solvent. The etching process takes hours or days, depending on the mineral sample. The solvent enlarges the fission tracks so that they become visible when viewed through a microscope. The tracks may number from none or very few to many thousands per square centimeter of surface. To determine a sample's history, one first counts the number of tracks over a known surface area. This number is related to the length of time during which the tracks have accumulated. Next, the number of remaining, undecayed uranium-238 atoms within the sample is measured by one of several techniques. The most popular is called the *external detector method*. The sample is irradiated with neutrons inside a nuclear reactor to quickly induce the fission of many additional uranium-238 atoms. The new fission tracks which result are captured in a target material placed closely adjacent to the original sample. The counting of these induced tracks gives a measure of the concentration of U-238 atoms in the sample prior to irradiation. Knowing this total and the number of original fission tracks is somewhat equivalent to knowing the numbers of daughter atoms and remaining parent atoms. From this data an age can be determined for the sample. Induced fission tracks can be very numerous, often measuring in the tens of millions per square centimeter. The actual counting is done with a microscope over a much smaller area.

RATE FISSION TRACK RESEARCH

Fission tracks provide valuable information for the RATE studies. In particular, the tracks provide verification that a large amount of nuclear decay has taken place in mineral samples. Particular rock samples were selected for the RATE fission track study based on their relationship to the Genesis flood. As described in the previous chapter, pre-Flood, mid-Flood, and late-Flood/post-Flood rocks are broadly correlated with the Precambrian, Paleozoic-Mesozoic, and Cenozoic eras. Twelve rock samples were obtained for RATE fission track analysis from the second and third categories. All are from the Grand Canyon-Colorado Plateau region. In each case the rock type is known as *tuff* and is composed of volcanic ash which has been cemented to a solid. Some of these tuff deposits cover extensive areas. It is the zircon crystals found within these tuff units that lend themselves readily to fission track counting.

The lower entries in Table 6-1 are Middle Cambrian from the lowest portion of the Paleozoic Era. These tuff deposits occur within Mauv Limestone (MT-2, MT-3 samples) and Tapeats Sandstone (TT-1 sample). The RATE samples collected were typically 3–5 kilograms in size, or 6–11 pounds. The next six tuff samples in Table 6-1 are labeled late Jurassic from the Mesozoic Era. The samples are taken from the Morrison Formation. This rock unit covers an extensive part of the western interior of the United States. It is famous for preserving fossil dinosaur bones in locations like Dinosaur National Monument in Utah. The upper three entries in Table 6-1 are taken from an ash layer called Peach Springs Tuff. This major ash deposit may originally have covered an area of 35,000 square kilometers. It extends over a distance of 350 km, or over 200 miles. In places, the tuff thickness is 70 meters, or 230 feet. The deposit is the result of a massive, historic volcanic

Table 6-1. (Right) Fission track age results for 12 tuff samples from the Grand Canyon-Colorado Plateau region. The number of grains in parenthesis show how many separate zircons were analyzed for fission tracks for each tuff sample. The previously published ages and RATE age results are all in millions of years, or Ma. The references are given in the technical RATE volumes (Vardiman et al., 2000, 2005).

THOUSANDS . . . NOT BILLIONS

RATE Ages (Ma)

Sample Name (Number of grains)	Location	Published Ages (Ma)	Youngest Measured	Best Estimate	Oldest Measured
Cenozoic *- Early Miocene*					
PST-1(20)	Snaggletooth area, CA	18.7 ± 1.5	17.0 ± 4.6	24.6 ± 1.2	34.5 ± 15.2
PST-2(20)	Kingman, AZ	17.3 ± 0.4	16.4 ± 3.7	20.9 ± 0.9	27.3 ± 5.2
PST-3(20)	"	18.5 ± 0.2	17.3 ± 2.2	20.9 ± 0.8	29.3 ± 4.9
Mesozoic *- Late Jurassic*					
NMF-64(20)	Notom, UT	106 ± 6	93.1 ± 18.7	132 ± 10	651.3 ± 210.4
NMF-49(9)	"	141 ± 6 145 ± 13 142 ± 6	113.6 ± 42.0	183.4 ± 20.8	343.1 ± 145.4
BMF-14(20)	Blanding area, UT		98.2 ± 16.7	144 ± 10	689.9 ± 187.6
BMF-28(19)			104.2 ± 22.3	136 ± 6	592.3 ± 137.4
MMF-1(20)	Montezuma Creek, UT	147.6 ± 0.8 149.2 ± 0.4	87.6 ± 15.4	137 ± 9	1,036.2 ± 309.8
MMF-4(18)		149.4 ± 0.7 149.8 ± 0.3	114.6 ± 18.6	148.7 ± 7.0	233.5 ± 46.3
Paleozoic *- Middle Cambrian*					
MT-2(20)	Grand Canyon, AZ		34.9 ± 7.2	62 ± 4	611.2 ± 254.9
MT-3(23)		535 ± 48	68.4 ± 8.3	74.6 ± 3.9	473.5 ± 150.5
TT-1(20)	"	563 ± 49	48.0 ± 14.9	75 ± 7	914.3 ± 414.8

eruption in the Southwest United States. The three Peach Springs Tuff samples labeled *PST* in the table are conventionally dated at about 20 million years old and placed in the early Miocene epoch. This is a portion of the Tertiary Period which is in turn part of the Cenozoic Era (Table 3-1).

The fission track dating of the RATE samples was contracted out to a commercial laboratory with world-class expertise in fission track analysis. GeoTrack International Laboratory, located in Melbourne, Australia, was selected for the work. There are many steps to the process. Samples are crushed, and then the zircon crystals are extracted, ground, polished, and etched. After counting the original fission tracks, neutron irradiation of the sample induces additional tracks. Each of these steps is carried out in an environment carefully monitored for contamination. Figure 6-1 is a photograph of uranium-238 fission tracks in grains of zircon. These tracks are from a RATE sample analyzed by GeoTrack International.

Figure 6-1. Photograph of hundreds of fission tracks in two side-by-side zircon grains. The microscopic black fission tracks are about 15 microns long. This is about one-tenth the thickness of a human hair. The photograph is courtesy of Pat Kelly of GeoTrack International.

RATE FISSION TRACK RESULTS

Table 6-1 summarizes the RATE fission track results. As an example of the data, consider the sample MT-3. This tuff is found in the middle section of the Mauv limestone in the Grand Canyon. There were 23 individual grains of zircon chosen from the rock for fission track analysis. The previously published age for this rock formation is 535 ± 48 million years. The uncertainty is ± 2 standard deviations as explained in chapter 3. Most of the published dates in the table are derived from earlier fission track data. The RATE ages for MT-3 varied between 68.4 million and 473.5 million years with the best estimate or "most likely value" from the fission track data giving 74.6 million years. A large amount of effort and data are summarized in Table 6-1. With multiple zircon grains analyzed for each sample, as shown in the parentheses, there were a total of 229 separate fission track measurements.

The fission track data tells us several things. First, notice the wide spread in the RATE age results for the Middle Cambrian samples. Also, the RATE ages fail to agree with previously published results, showing major disagreement or discordance. The reason may be related to the thermal histories of the samples. Fission track dates do not give the full geologic age of a sample but instead give the cooling age, that is, the time since the rock cooled below its annealing temperature. The younger dates may indicate these zircon grains were reset to zero fission track age by a subsequent heating event. There may be a correlation with the tectonic ground movement in the area that uplifted the Colorado Plateau.

On the other hand, the Middle Cambrian results confirm that substantial spontaneous decay of uranium-238 has occurred in these rocks. In fact, the previously published values indicate as much as 500 million years of decay. In the young-earth view, the Middle Cambrian rocks were deposited during the early stages of the Flood. This implies that greatly accelerated nuclear decay occurred at this time, including the spontaneous fission of uranium-238 to form the observed tracks. During the Flood there was also global tectonic activity occurring with associated heating effects which may have erased many fission tracks as well as radiohalos.

The RATE fission track ages determined for the Late Jurassic and Early Miocene reveal no surprises. All are in close agreement with the published ages. This is not to say that the RATE team agrees with the conventional assumptions from which these large ages are derived. Instead, we note that the amount of spontaneous uranium-238 fission is in close agreement with the amount of uranium alpha decay as determined by other methods, at least for the Jurassic and Miocene samples. We conclude that the accelerated decay implied by helium diffusion and polonium radiohalos is consistent with a similar amount of accelerated fission decay in these rocks.

FISSION TRACK SUMMARY

Fission tracks and radiohalos (chapter 5) provide a visible microscopic record of nuclear decay in crystalline solids. In the young-earth view, these fingerprints give evidence for accelerated decay, especially during the Genesis flood event. In addition, the abundance of fission tracks and radiohalos provide evidence for a recent creation. This follows because the host rocks have not experienced serious heating since the track and halo formation. Just hundreds of degrees are sufficient to erase the crystal defects, yet they remain. It is difficult to imagine the rock formations remaining cool over vast ages of time with accompanying episodes of volcanic and tectonic activity. In the young-earth view, the radiohalos and tracks remain relatively recent and freshly made.

Chapter 7

DISCORDANT RADIOISOTOPE DATES

Research by Steven Austin

SELECTIVITY OF RADIOISOTOPE DATA

Geologists have published many thousands of reports on rock ages based on radioisotope studies. It is impossible to evaluate this large volume of data in comprehensive detail. In addition, questions naturally arise for which answers are not readily available. For example, how and why were particular rock samples chosen for analysis and reporting? When the rock ages were determined, were selected results published and others held back? This is not to imply that the geologic literature is dishonest. However, we all filter data through a grid of prior assumptions. This unavoidable bias in the selection and interpretation of data has been called the *file drawer problem*. That is, data which give unexpected or inconsistent results may be stored away in a file drawer for later investigation rather than being published. This can occur in all disciplines, including geology, where the approximate age of a rock formation is assumed to correspond to its location in the geologic record.

Although some bias in reported dates is unavoidable, there is often close agreement reported from several independent dating methods which all give an ancient age for a particular rock formation. This consistency or concordance of radioisotope dating results has been perceived as a significant challenge to the young-earth model. If the ages determined by these multiple methods are in error, then why do they agree with one another? To address this question, the RATE team conducted its own study of radioisotope dating by applying multiple radioisotope methods to fresh rock samples. These samples were collected and thoroughly documented relative to their geologic setting. Following careful sample preparation they were sent to multiple, state-of-the-art commercial radioisotope dating laboratories. The results show clearly that discordance exists among the various radioisotope dating methods. This discordance is systematic and repeatable for rock samples from different geologic locations and settings.

RATE SAMPLE COLLECTION

Two particular locations were selected for the collection of RATE rock samples. Both sites are understood by geologists to date from Precambrian time (Table 3-1). The first site is in the Beartooth Mountains of northwest Wyoming near Yellowstone National Park. This region is believed to contain some of the oldest rocks in the United States, with a conventional age of nearly 3 billion years. A single, multi-kilogram sample of rock was collected at this location. The formation is a large rock body, tens of meters in size and identified as amphibolite. This is a dark-colored type of rock formed from the metamorphism of the fine-grained volcanic rock called *andesite*. The sample is considered to be representative of many similar metamorphic rock formations. It was collected at an elevation of 10,200 feet where the rock had been exposed during highway excavation. This location was chosen because it is the same site sampled in several previously published radioisotope studies.

The second collection site chosen for detailed radioisotope study was a diabase sill located at Bass Rapids in the central portion of Arizona's Grand Canyon. Figure 7-1 shows the location of this sill in the lowermost portion of the canyon's rock strata. A sill forms when magma intrudes between existing layers of rock strata and then cools and solidifies. The word *diabase* refers to a type of igneous rock with the composition of basalt which has visible mineral crystals. As the temperature decreases within a molten sill, individual component mineral grains begin to appear. These minerals sink downward due to gravity settling and so the mineral composition within the sill varies, with a distinct lighter colored layer on top. The Bass Rapids sill ranges in thickness from 20 to 200 meters (65–655 feet). This sill is a particularly good candidate for investigation because of its many previous geochemical and radioisotope studies, more than for any other sill in the Grand Canyon. Also, on a practical level, the sill is well defined with many accessible outcrop exposures.

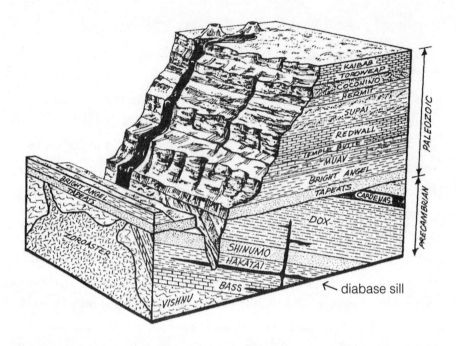

Figure 7-1. Drawing of a portion of the Grand Canyon. Notice the diabase sill (black streaks) in the lowermost portion of the canyon. Rock from this sill was sampled for radioisotope study.

ROCK SAMPLE PREPARATION

Portions of the Beartooth rock sample were crushed and then ground to a fine powder using an iron mortar. Six distinct minerals were separated from the resulting powder mixture. This was accomplished by placing the powder samples into a series of dense liquids in which some minerals float and others sink. The liquids were diluted to produce precisely calibrated densities. A laboratory centrifuge also was used to separate and concentrate the minerals. The resulting isolated minerals were quartz, plagioclase, biotite, hornblende, magnetite, and titanite, also called *sphene*. The reason for this mineral separation procedure is to be able to apply the mineral isochron method described in chapter 2. The minerals incorporate different concentrations of the various parent radioisotopes as they crystallize from the magma. The mineral isochron method is an especially sensitive way to compare the consistency of the various parent-daughter radioisotope methods on a single sample of rock. The separation of distinct minerals from a rock sample is a tedious process which is not frequently done because of the time, effort, and cost involved.

At the Bass Rapids sill in the Grand Canyon, 11 rock samples were collected. They came from various exposed levels of the sill, ranging from near the top to 85 meters downward. One of the sill rock specimens produced 11 distinct minerals for study, an impressive accomplishment. The mineral powders were commercially analyzed by x-ray diffraction and optical microscopy to assure their proper purity and identification.

Thin rock sections were also prepared from the samples. The steps involve cutting a chip of about one centimeter square from the rock and mounting it with glue on a glass slide. The chip is then ground down until very thin. It is further polished with fine powders until its thickness is 30 microns. At this stage, the ultra-thin rock section becomes transparent to light. Under a microscope with a polarizing filter, the component minerals of the rock show up with distinct patterns and colors. The thin sections of rock reveal the relative amounts of each mineral, as well as their chemistry and texture.

Beartooth Mountains Sample Results

All the whole rock samples, and also the separate minerals, were analyzed using four radioisotope pairs. These include the isotopes potassium-argon (K-Ar), rubidium-strontium (Rb-Sr), samarium-neodymium (Sm-Nd), and lead-lead (Pb-Pb). The counting procedures were contracted out by RATE to commercial laboratories located in Colorado, Massachusetts, and Ontario, Canada. All the data were plotted on isochron graphs and statistically analyzed with the widely used computer software program *Isoplot*. The output of the program includes the isochron age. This value simply reflects the radioisotope input data and several assumptions, including unchanging nuclear decay rates in the past.

The Beartooth Mountains rock unit was dated previously at 2,790 ± 35 million years using rubidium-strontium isotopes (Wooden et al., 1982). The plus or minus margin of uncertainty is as described in chapter 3 in terms of ± 2 standard deviations. The ± 35 million years represents the uncertainty of the calculated age due to the scatter of the data points on the isochron graph.

Table 7-1 summarizes the RATE results for the Beartooth Mountains site. All the numbers shown are in millions of years. The right column in the table indicates whether the isochron data points were derived from distinct minerals or from the rock as a whole. It is found that for particular isochron graphs, there is often an extraordinary close fit of the data points to a straight line. At the same time, however, Table 7-1 also shows significant scatter in the ages obtained for the various minerals and also between the isotope methods. Yet all these age results were derived from a single rock. The following section summarizes several possible types of discordance.

CATEGORIES OF DISCORDANCE

Rock sample ages are said to be *concordant* when there is close agreement between distinct radioisotope methods. In contrast, if multiple results for a rock sample disagree with each other in age they are said to be *discordant*. Four categories of discordance are defined here, each based on the ages derived from isochron graphs:

1. When multiple samples are taken from the same rock formation, they are cogenetic and should have closely similar ages. If the results disagree, they are discordant.

2. The age of the whole rock should be the average of that found for its component minerals. The second category of

Table 7-1. Radioisotope dating results for mineral and whole rock samples from the Beartooth Mountains of Wyoming. All the listed ages are based on isochron plots and are given in millions of years, ie, 2,011 = 2,011,000,000 years. The ages are based on the uniformitarian assumption of unchanging nuclear decay rates in the past. The last column shows the type of data used for each isochron.

	Conventional Age	
Dating Isotopes	**(Millions of Years)**	**Type of Data**
Potassium-Argon	1,520 ± 31	Quartz-plagioclase mineral
	2,011 ± 45	Whole rock
	2,403 ± 53	Biotite mineral
	2,620 ± 53	Hornblende mineral
Rubidium-Strontium	2,515 ± 110	5 Minerals
	2,790 ± 35	Previously published result based on 30 whole rock samples (Wooden et al., 1982)
Samarium-Neodymium	2,886 ± 190	4 Minerals
Lead-Lead	2,689 ± 9	5 Minerals

discordance occurs when the whole rock age is greater than that of its constituent minerals.

3. Two or more discordant dates may result for minerals which have been separated from the same rock.

4. In contrast to category two, a whole rock age may be less than that determined for the minerals taken from the same rock.

Table 7-1 reveals that the RATE data for the Beartooth rock sample shows discordance in all four of the defined categories. In some cases, the whole rock age is greater than the age of the minerals, and for others, the reverse occurs. The potassium-argon mineral results vary between 1,520 and 2,620 million years. Also, the mineral isochron for rubidium-strontium gives an age of 2,515 ± 110 million years while the samarium-neodymium method for the same minerals gives an age of 2,886 ± 190 million years, a substantial difference of 371 million years. The most likely explanation for these discordant results will be explored following the Bass Rapids sill discussion.

BASS RAPIDS SILL RESULTS

The 11 Grand Canyon rock samples were prepared using procedures similar to those used for the Beartooth Mountains rock. They were dated commercially using the most advanced radioisotope technology. The Bass Rapids RATE results for the several radioisotopes applied are presented in Table 7-2. As before, the derived ages are expressed in millions of years. The generally accepted age for this formation is 1,070 million years (Elston and McKee, 1982). Clearly, the RATE results diverge considerably from this value. At the same time, however, as with the Beartooth results, there is excellent agreement between the data points for each particular isochron graph as shown by the relatively small ± uncertainties. One of the samarium-neodymium mineral isochrons is shown for illustration in Figure 7-2.

Table 7-2 again shows discordance in all four of the defined categories, just as shown in Table 7-1. Especially noteworthy is the whole rock potassium-argon age of 841.5 ± 164 million years while samarium-neodymium gives 1,379 ± 140 million years, equating to a large-scale difference of 537.5 million years.

DISCORDANCE AT OTHER LOCATIONS

Discordant dates similar to those found by RATE are also reported for many other sites in the geologic literature. Three examples dated as

THOUSANDS . . . NOT BILLIONS

Table 7-2. Radioisotope dating results for a single rock sample from the Bass Rapids sill in the Grand Canyon. All ages are computed from isochron plots and are in millions of years. The ages are based on the conventional assumption of unchanging nuclear decay rates in the past. The last column shows the type of data used for each isochron.

Conventional Age		
Dating Isotopes	**(In Millions of Years)**	**Type of Data**
Potassium-Argon	841.5 ± 164	11 Whole rock samples
	656 ± 15 to 1,053 ± 24	Model ages from single whole rocks
Rubidium- Strontium	1,007 ± 79	Magnetite mineral grains from 7 rock samples
	1,055 ± 46	11 Whole rock
	1,060 ± 24	7 Minerals
	1,070 ± 30	Previously published age based on 5 whole rock samples (Elston and McKee, 1982)
	1,075 ± 34	12 Minerals
Lead-Lead	1,250 ± 130	11 Whole rock
	1,327 ± 230	6 Minerals
Samarium-Neodymium	1,330 ± 360	8 Minerals
	1,336 ± 380	Magnetite mineral grains from 7 rock samples
	1,379 ± 140	6 Minerals

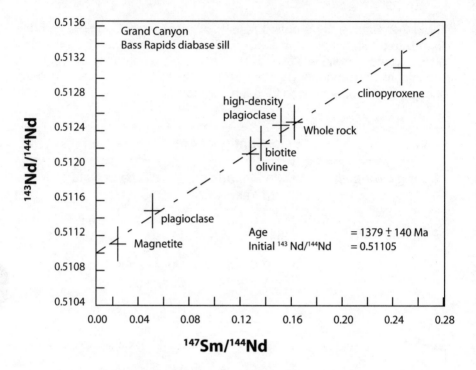

Figure 7-2. An example RATE isochron for the rock sample from the Bass Rapids sill in the Grand Canyon. The data points are the samarium-neodymium isotope components for six mineral fractions and also the whole-rock measurement. The small crosses show error margins of the measurements which are ± 2 standard deviations. The isochron mineral age from the slope of the isochron is 1,379 ± 140 million years. The initial Nd-143/Nd-144 ratio from the intercept on the vertical axis is 0.51105.

Precambrian from widely separated locations will be mentioned here. The first is called the Great Dike rock formation located in Zimbabwe, Africa. This is a much-studied narrow intrusion of molten rock which forced its way into existing rock and then solidified. It was later exposed by erosion. The volcanic rock covers more than 3,000 square kilometers (1,160 square miles). The maximum thickness of this formation exceeds 3,500 meters, or 2.1 miles. Radioisotope dating results reported in 1998 yield an age for the Great Dike more than 100 million years older

THOUSANDS . . . NOT BILLIONS

than the previously established rubidium-strontium isochron age of 2,455 ± 16 million years. The new dating results come from Sm-Nd, U-Pb, and Pb-Pb methods. The conclusion is that the accuracy of rubidium-strontium dating is suspect. A discrepancy of one hundred million years is not a trivial time difference.

Similar discordant isochron ages are obtained for the Stuart Dike swarm located in south-central Australia. A dike swarm is a multitude of magma eruptions which occurred simultaneously in the same general region. The Australian ages are found to vary between 897 ± 9 and 1,076 ± 33 million years, both dates resulting from rubidium-strontium dating.

Finally, a dike swarm in Uruguay, South America, yields discordant dates ranging from 1,366 ± 18 to 1,766 ± 124 million years, again using the rubidium-strontium method. In each of these cases, the separate isochron plots give straight lines with very consistent data. Such an alignment of data suggests accurate dates, yet the results between the isochrons are notably discordant. This discordance means that interpretation is required to select which results might be trustworthy. It also hints that some deeper explanation is needed for radioisotope results.

POSSIBLE EXPLANATIONS OF DISCORDANCE

There are several possible explanations for the discordant isotope dating results. Three major possibilities will be given here. First, there may be a mixing of isotopes between the magma and the rock body into which the magma intrudes. This possibility is discussed in the next chapter, but suffice it to say that there are ways to determine whether or not this indeed has occurred. Second, it has been suggested that the separate minerals in a sill may solidify at significantly different times. Thus, one mineral may form and start to age, while other minerals remain molten with zero age until millions of years later. Such a process would indeed lead to discordance between mineral samples from the sill. However, there is no evidence that magma cooling and solidifying takes place at such an incredibly slow pace.

The third possible reason for discordant dates is that the decay rates of the radioisotopes have been different in the past than they are today. Although this idea usually is not considered, it may provide the best explanation for the results reported in this chapter. Suppose nuclear decay was accelerated in the past but by unequal factors for the various isotopes. Then the measured radioisotope ages would be discordant. What effect would an acceleration of decay have on isochron plots? As Figure 2-1 shows, the isochron line swings upward as daughter isotopes accumulate within samples. However, the isochron will look the same regardless of the rate of nuclear decay. It is the total amount of decay that determines the slope of the isochron line, not the rate of decay. However, suppose the various isotopes experienced different amounts of accelerated decay in the past. This would lead to discordance among the radioisotope methods.

SIGNIFICANT TRENDS

Figure 7-3 gives a summary view of the four radioisotope results for the Bass Rapids sill in the Grand Canyon. Keep in mind that the sill must actually have one true age. However, the ages derived from isochron plots vary between 841.5 million years (potassium-argon) and 1,379 million years (samarium-neodymium). The figure shows an interesting trend. The isochron ages for the sill are greater for the alpha decay isotopes (U-238, Sm-147) than for those that undergo beta decay (K-40, Rb-87). This suggests that during a past period of accelerated decay, the alpha decay process underwent more overall decay than the beta process. There also is a second, more tentative, trend noticed in Figure 7-3 whereby isotopes with a longer half-life tend to give greater ages for rocks. Samarium-147 has the longest half-life of the four parent isotopes and also gives the oldest age for the Bass Rapids sill. This second trend can alternately be related to atomic

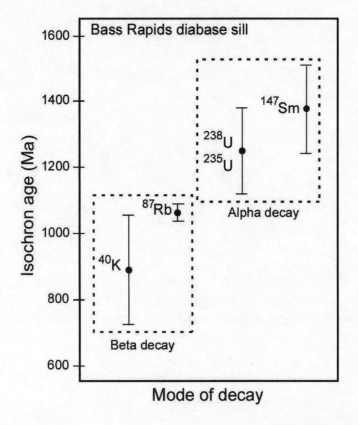

Figure 7-3. A summary of alpha and beta radiation trends for four isotope systems dating the Bass Rapids diabase sill in the Grand Canyon. All four data points shown result from the same rock sample. The alpha emitters give older ages than the beta emitters.

weight: heavier radioisotopes such as samarium and uranium tend to give older ages. The trends are also evident in the discordant dating results mentioned previously from Zimbabwe, Australia, and Uruguay. According to the conventional assumption of unchanging nuclear decay rates, such trends should not exist since all four data points in Figure 7-3 represent the same geological event. The trends eventually may prove helpful in identifying the actual mechanism by which nuclear decay processes were altered in the past.

Chapter 8

RADIOISOTOPE DATING
CASE STUDIES

Research by Andrew Snelling

FURTHER ROCK SAMPLING

The previous chapter describes two case studies involving detailed radioisotope dating of Precambrian rock formations. The locations are the Beartooth Mountains of Wyoming and Arizona's Grand Canyon. For both sites there were several varieties of disagreement or discordance in the calculated isochron ages. This occurs even though many sets of the data points yield straight lines on individual isochron plots with little scatter and good statistics. When isochrons display such properties, it is often taken as assurance that the radioisotope dates are reliable.

The RATE team saw value in extending the radioisotope case studies to additional sites. These should again include Precambrian age rocks but also several formations of more recent age. Answers were sought regarding three questions. First, does the discordance of dates continue as a general trend or were the results of the previous chapter actually exceptions to a general pattern of concordance? Second, if discordance of dates again arises, does the trend shown in Figure 7-3 also persist? If it does, this will count as additional evidence that nuclear decay rates have been different in the past. The third question asks whether physical explanations can be identified for the discordant dates.

SAMPLE LOCATIONS

Rock samples were collected and documented from ten locations. In each case, the rocks were carefully selected as representative of the particular site. The choice was made to focus on one type of rock to simplify the data comparison. Almost all the samples came from basaltic or mafic rock units. The origin of this rock is magma from the mantle. The word *mafic* (măf′ic) identifies two major element components: magnesium and iron (*ferrum* in Latin). *Basalt* refers to the dark, fine-grained igneous rock that is very common across the earth where magma formed by the partial melting of mantle rock has risen to the surface as lava. It commonly flows for a considerable distance and cools rapidly. Basalt is found in volcanic areas, on the floor of the ocean, and also on the moon's surface. The ten rock units are listed in the first column of Table 8-1. The following are brief location descriptions with definitions for some of the geologic names appearing in the table.

Mount Ngauruhoe is located on the North Island of New Zealand and is one of the country's most active volcanoes. As a point of interest, Mount Ngauruhoe is featured in the popular *Lord of the Rings* movie trilogy as Mount Doom. Eleven samples of andesite were taken from solidified lava which flowed at Mount Ngauruhoe just decades ago. Andesite is a dark volcanic rock named for the Andes Mountains where it is also found. Many volcanic peaks consist largely of andesite.

In the Grand Canyon, the Uinkaret Plateau collection site is another region of "recent" volcanic flows, dated at less than one million years old. On the edge of the canyon's north rim there are about 160 volcanic cones comprising the Uinkaret Volcanic Field (Figure 7-1). Uinkaret is a Paiute Indian word meaning "place of the pines." Some of the eruptions must have been a spectacular sight for any Native Americans who happened to be in the vicinity. In the evolutionary view, of course, modern man had not yet evolved, but the creation position is not limited by this constraint. The lavas swept directly over the edge of the canyon and fell a mile downward as fiery cascades. Some of this lava temporarily blocked the flow of the Colorado River, flooding parts of the canyon. Ten basalt samples were gathered by permission from the National Park Service.

The Somerset Dam rock samples come from near Brisbane along Australia's east coast. Basalt magma intruded into preexisting rock and then solidified to gabbro. In conventional geology this event is dated over 200 million years ago (Table 8-1). Gabbro forms underground from magma which is low in silica, or SiO_2. The exposed portion of the

Table 8-1. Radioisotope data for ten sites. The samples include basaltic and metamorphic rock varieties. All the ages are given in millions of years and are based on the uniformitarian assumption of unchanging decay rates.

Rock Unit	Location	Conventional Age	Model Ages K-Ar Min.	Model Ages K-Ar Max.	Whole Rock Isochron Ages K-Ar	Rb-Sr	Sm-Nd	Pb-Pb
Recent Mt. Ngauruhoe Andesite	New Zealand	Historic 1949, 1954, 1975	<0.27	3.5±0.2	-	133±87(7)	197±160(5)	3,908±390(7)
Uinkaret Plateau Basalt	Western Grand Canyon, AZ	<1.16±0.18	1.19±0.18	20.7±1.3	-	1,143±220(7)	916±570(6)	-
Mesozoic Somerset Dam Gabbro	Queensland, Australia	216±4 225±2.3	182.7±9	252.8±9	174±81(15)	393±170(14)	259±76(13)	1,425±1,000(13)
Precambrian Cardenas Basalt	Eastern Grand Canyon, AZ	1,103±66	577±12	1,013±37	516±30(14)	892±82(22) 1,111±81(19)	1,588±170(8)	1,385±950(4)
Bass Rapids Diabase Sill	Grand Canyon, AZ	1,070±30	656±15	1,053±24	841.5±164	1,007±79(7) 1,055±46(11) 1,060±24(7) 1,075±34(12)	1,330±360(9) 1,336±380(7) 1,379±140(7)	1,250±130(11) 1,327±230(6) 1,584±420(10)

RATE Age Results (Millions of Years)

THOUSANDS . . . NOT BILLIONS

Apache Group Basalt	Central AZ	1,100	513±13	968.9±25	–	2,295±300(5)	–	1,304±69(18)
Apache Group Diabase Sill	Central AZ	1,120±10 1,140±40	267.5±14	855.8±17	–	2,067±380(16)	–	1,142±98(19) 1,146±59(18)
Brahma Amphibolite	Grand Canyon, AZ	1,740-1,750	405.1±10	2,574.2±73	–	840±86(25) 1,240±84(19)	1,655±40(21) 1,678±60(24)	1,864±78(27) 1,883±53(20)
Elves Chasm Granodiorite	Grand Canyon, AZ	1,840±1-	–	–	–	1,512±140(7)	1,664±200(7)	1,933±220(7)
Beartooth Amphibolite	Northeast WY	2,790±35	1,520±31	2,620±53	–	2,515±110(5)	2,886±190(4)	2,689.4±8.6(5)

gabbro covers about 4 square kilometers or 1.4 mi². A total of 18 samples were gathered.

Six of the Precambrian sites are in Arizona, including the Grand Canyon. Dozens of samples were collected within the canyon, again by permission. Other rocks were already on hand from earlier research field trips. The Cardenas Basalt is a series of volcanic layers with a maximum thickness of nearly 1,000 feet (305 meters). These were lavas which flowed from volcanoes which have now eroded away. The related diabase sills are geologic structures which result when magma intrudes between existing rock layers and then cools in place. Sills are typically tens of meters thick, that is, 30 or more feet. Diabase is a fine-textured, dark-colored basaltic igneous rock which has cooled underground.

Amphibolite is rock which results from the metamorphism of basalt. It often has a dark reflective appearance. Amphibolite formations appear in the lowermost portions of the Grand Canyon. Their location and description were first reported by canyon pioneer John Wesley Powell in 1876. Figure 8-1 is an early drawing of the north wall of the Grand Canyon. This picture first appeared in Powell's report of his explorations of the Colorado River (Powell, 1969).

Granodiorite is a common rock with speckles of mineral grains including quartz, feldspar, biotite, and hornblende. It is a granite which forms at some depth underground. Granodiorite is not mafic like the other samples, but the Elves Chasm samples are added to this

Figure 8-1. Illustration of the lowermost north wall of the Grand Canyon. This drawing appeared in John Wesley Powell's 1875 report of explorations of the Colorado River (Powell reprint, 1969). Closest to the river are igneous rocks which underlie the stratified layers. Elves Chasm rock, listed in Table 8-1, is part of the lower crystalline rock. See also Figure 7-1.

study because they are considered some of the oldest rocks in the entire Canyon.

In central and south Arizona there are extensive sedimentary strata, sills, and basalt flows. Thirty rock samples were collected from the Apache Group flows and sills. Portions of these are exposed by excavations along Arizona highways.

The sample from the Beartooth Mountains of Wyoming is described in the previous chapter. This Precambrian rock is placed at the end of Table 8-1. It has by far the oldest conventional date of the ten sites studied. Its analysis is repeated in this chapter for comparison purposes.

RATE SAMPLE ANALYSIS

Rock samples are carefully handled when they are to be used for isotope dating experiments. To avoid possible surface contamination, outside portions are removed using a lapidary saw. Thin sections are prepared for microscope identification of the rock's component minerals. The interior portion of each rock is then washed, dried, and crushed to powder. The resulting grains are sorted using sieves to obtain uniform size particles.

Several commercial laboratories were contracted to analyze the samples chemically and to date them from their radioisotope content. Laboratories were typically provided with 20–50 grams of each sample. As in the earlier case studies, several radioisotope methods were applied including potassium-argon (K-Ar), rubidium-strontium (Rb-Sr), samarium-neodymium (Sm-Nd), and lead-lead (Pb-Pb). Whole rock isochron plots were generated for all of the radioisotope data. Mineral isochrons were also prepared for the Bass Rapids and Beartooth samples. In addition to the potassium-argon isochron dates, model ages were obtained for several individual rock samples. These K-Ar model ages provide a useful comparison with the isochron ages which are multi-sample averages.

RADIOISOTOPE RESULTS

The measured ages of the samples are summarized in Table 8-1. The first two columns identify the ten rock units and their locations. Each of these rock formations has been thoroughly studied by geologists and described in the literature. The third column lists the published conventional ages. Notice the age range from very recent at the top of the list, Mount Ngauruhoe, to nearly three billion years at the bottom for the Beartooth Mountains sample. All of the radioisotope age RATE results in the table are listed in millions of years. The measured range of the potassium-argon whole rock model ages is listed in terms of minimum and maximum. The ± uncertainties represent a two standard deviation spread in ages that should encompass over 95 percent of any repeated measurements. All the results for Rb-Sr, Sm-Nd, and Pb-Pb are whole rock isochron ages. The numbers in parentheses after the dates show the number of samples measured and plotted on the isochrons.

INTERPRETATION OF THE RADIOISOTOPE RESULTS

Several general conclusions follow from the RATE data shown in Table 8-1.

1. A marked discordance is found among the different isochron methods for many of the samples, particularly for the seven Precambrian sites. The Brahma amphibolite samples, for example, range between 840 million years (Rb-Sr) and 1,864 million years (Pb-Pb). This is a difference of 122 percent.

2. The potassium-argon dates show an especially wide variation. The oldest two Precambrian sites, Elves Chasm in the Grand Canyon and the Beartooth Mountains, did not produce statistically useable K-Ar isochrons. There was too much scatter of the plotted data points to draw an isochron

line. These findings imply widespread contamination of the K-Ar radioisotopes by open-system behavior in the rock samples.

3. There are some missing isochron dates in Table 8-1. This occurs because either the data points are too closely grouped to draw an isochron line, or else a wide scatter of the data points does not define a usable isochron line.

4. Some of the isochron dates in Table 8-1 have large ± uncertainties. These dates are statistically questionable because of the problems listed in point 3. An isochron line was established for these samples, but not with statistical confidence.

5. Other than the isochrons just described, the other plots are tightly constrained with large numbers of data points and excellent statistics. This is especially true of the Brahma amphibolites. At the same time, however, the three amphibolite ages derived from Rb-Sr, Sm-Nd, and Pb-Pb dating are highly discordant. This raises a cautionary flag in accepting any isochron date in isolation, even when it shows impressive statistics.

6. There is a repeat of the pattern of variation for alpha and beta decays noticed earlier for the Bass Rapids sill and shown in Figure 7-3. The alpha-decay radioisotopes (U-238, U-235, Sm-147) consistently give older isochron ages than the beta-decay radioisotopes (K-40, Rb-87) when dating the same geologic event. Also, heavier isotopes tend to give older dates. These general trends continue for the Cardenas Basalt lavas, the Brahma amphibolites, and the Elves Chasm Granodiorite. This pattern of discordance is less evident for the Uinkaret Plateau basalt. The implication is that for some interval in the past, alpha decay proceeded at a rate different from that of beta decay, relative to present rates.

INHERITANCE OF RADIOISOTOPES

Some magma bodies begin their journey upward toward the earth's surface from the upper mantle, 10–40 miles below ground. Other magma begins as pockets or chambers of melted rock well above the mantle and within the crust. Magma is less dense than the overlying rock due to its high temperature, chemical makeup, and dissolved gases. These factors give the magma buoyancy as it ascends through existing rock strata, either slowly or rapidly. The underground appearance of this moving molten plume might resemble a large distorted bubble, similar to the rising globule in a lava lamp. The magma may eventually cease its upward movement and cool underground to form solid rock. Alternatively, the magma may arrive at the surface of the earth and erupt as lava. There is evidence that the melting process that forms the magma does not necessarily exclude daughter atoms that existed in the source rock from which the magma formed. The daughter isotopes can be incorporated into the magma and carried along within the moving mass. These isotopes then later become part of the resulting rock formation when the magma cools. As a result, these rocks will yield ages older than they actually are. There is uncertainty here because we do not know how much of the total measured radioisotope decay occurred before formation of the rock.

Notice the ages measured for the two sites of recent origin in Table 8-1. These include the lava flows from the New Zealand volcano and also from the Uinkaret Plateau at the Grand Canyon. The ages for Mount Ngauruhoe rocks include about 3.5 million years from potassium-argon, and more than a hundred million years from rubidium-strontium and samarium-neodymium. In the case of potassium-argon it is clear that considerable argon-40 was already present in this lava when it cooled. Some of this argon undoubtedly was inherited from the mantle source rocks of the magma. Another component likely comes from crustal mixing as described in the next section. For the lead-lead dating of Mount Ngauruhoe rocks, we observe an age of 3,908 million years versus a true age of just 50 years. This is a discrepancy of 7.8 billion percent!

The RATE radioisotope studies reveal large-scale errors for volcanic rocks known to be less than a century old. Similar results have been previously published for many other modern lavas which yield exceedingly old ages. This is particularly true of basaltic lavas on ocean islands such as Hawaii. These young rocks commonly carry "ancient" radioisotope signatures inherited from their mantle sources.

How can we determine whether particular isotopes in rocks have been inherited from geochemical reservoirs in the mantle below? After all, we have never tapped directly into the mantle to test its chemistry. The crust-mantle boundary lies on average tens of kilometers beneath the surface and the deepest hole drilled into the earth to date is about 12 kilometers, or 7.5 miles. There is data available, however, concerning the isotopic composition of the mantle. This information comes from the analysis of thousands of samples of modern oceanic basalt worldwide. Since basalt is formed by the partial melting of mantle rock, these analyses provide isotope compositions or signatures directly from the mantle. From the isotope data in Table 8-1, one can construct isotope correlation diagrams. These are complex diagrams which simultaneously compare the ratios of several isotopes. Of special interest to these mantle studies are the elements strontium, neodymium, and lead. The isotope signatures from previous measurements imply the existence of several distinct mantle reservoirs or domains. The isotope correlation diagrams show how closely a rock sample in question matches these mantle reservoirs.

Isotope correlation diagrams were drawn for many of the RATE samples. Only the Somerset Dam site in Australia yields results suggesting that this rock intrusion is derived purely from the upper mantle. The other nine sites did not have isotope ratios closely matching known mantle compositions. For these samples, inheritance from a mantle source does not appear to be a sufficient explanation for observed discordance. This suggests that crustal material was probably mixed into the magma as it made its journey upward through the crustal rock from the mantle below. This mixing process is described in the next section. The procedure for matching the isotope pattern of a rock sample to possible mantle reservoirs is somewhat uncertain and is an area of active investigation with geologists. Understanding the variations in radioisotopes in the mantle is of special interest because of its connections with plate tectonics and seafloor spreading.

The previous mantle discussion is mainly limited to recently formed "modern" basalts. What about the abundant Precambrian basalts found all around the world? Might some of these also have formed by similar processes as we observe today? If so, then they also could have inherited much of their isotope signatures from the mantle. If this is the case, then these rocks also may reflect artificially old ages.

MIXING OF RADIOISOTOPES

The term *mixing* here refers to the open-system behavior of rocks that exchange radioisotopes and other trace elements with their surroundings. This may happen with magma before it cools or with solidified rock at a later time. One way this occurs is when magma moves upward through the crust and melts some of the surrounding rock. This newly melted crustal material can be assimilated or incorporated directly into the magma. Then when the magma cools and solidifies, the new rock contains isotopes from the melted crustal material. While moving upward, all magma must flow through crustal material or adjacent to it. One might therefore conclude that all igneous rocks are contaminated to some extent by mixing with nearby rock through which their magma has migrated. In locations where crustal mixing is recognizable, crustal material commonly amounts to 5–10 percent by volume of the magma. Mixing in magma from two or more different source regions can result in a mixture of isotopes that makes age determination quite difficult. To deal with this, there have been efforts by geologists to untangle the distinct ages that have been mixed or averaged in such situations. These efforts take the form of mixing models (Faure and Mensing, 2005). The goal is to separate mathematically the sample radioisotope measurements into two or more component materials and to determine their separate distinct ages. The results are rather arbitrary since the isotopes can be allocated in different ways.

Another potential source of rock component mixing involves the underground flow of heated water and gaseous fluids. At high pressure, water readily moves through rock pores and fissures and between mineral grains. The inevitable result is an exchange of ions or charged atoms along the fluid path. Geologists are still learning about the important role that these hydrothermal solutions play in many underground processes including granite formation, metamorphism, mineral crystal growth, metal ore deposits, and radiohalo development.

The RATE findings for the Grand Canyon Bass Rapids sill indicate a significant contribution by hydrothermal water to crustal mixing. Hot magma intruded between layers of sedimentary shale, and the adjacent shale was heated by the magma and converted to the metamorphic rock type called *hornfels*. Samples of this hornfels were collected and analyzed for their isotopic content. A close match was found in the amounts of several isotopes between the hornfels and the sill material. This was especially true for the dating isotope neodymium. The close agreement shows that there was indeed an exchange of elements between the sill magma and the host shale. Since the adjacent shale did not melt during its metamorphism, the chemical transfer must have been facilitated by the movement of abundant hydrothermal hot fluids through the rock.

The potassium-argon method is known to display open-system behavior. The daughter product, argon-40, is a gas. These argon atoms are inert and similar to helium. The argon does not combine chemically with other elements, and it remains highly mobile. In addition, argon-40 is readily available in the mantle and is also a common atmospheric gas. Argon comprises nearly 1 percent of the earth's atmosphere and 99.6 percent of this argon is the Ar-40 variety. The argon-40 from the air and from ground sources is identical to that formed by the decay of postassium-40. Either the loss or inheritance of Ar-40 is surely one reason why the maximum and minimum K-Ar ages shown in Table 8-1 vary so widely. The large range of ages occurred even in closely spaced cogenetic rock samples. Two of the Brahma amphibolite samples were located only 0.84 meters (33 inches) apart, yet their K-Ar dates are 1,205.3 ± 31 and 2,574.2 ± 73 million years. The second date is more than twice as old as the first.

The Bass Rapids site's potassium-argon isochron age is 841.5 ± 164 million years. The isochron line passes directly through the origin which implies no initial argon-40 contamination. However, the K-Ar model ages for the same site vary between 656 ± 15 and 1,053 ± 24 million years which shows considerable argon-40 contamination. These results illustrate the high level of uncertainty that is common in K-Ar dating.

The effects of inheritance and mixing do not necessarily reveal themselves in isochron diagrams. Figure 2-1 illustrates ideally how isochrons are supposed to identify initial daughter products in rock. Isochrons are also thought to show possible open-system contamination if the data points do not plot on a straight line. However, reality is not quite so simple. Even when a well-defined straight line does occur on a plot it may not be a true isochron. Instead, the alignment may be the result of mixing with crustal rock or inheritance from mantle material. When this occurs, the resulting isochron might better be called a *false isochron* or a *pseudoisochron* (Fauer and Mensing, 2005).

THE GEOLOGIC RECORD AND BIBLICAL HISTORY

As we have seen, there are multiple problems and uncertainties with the radioisotope ages of rocks. Nevertheless, there is a clear trend of relatively older rocks existing at deeper levels of strata. This can be seen in Table 8-1 by comparing the lowermost Precambrian rocks with the younger varieties. It is this pattern which leads to the construction of the geologic time record in Table 3-1.

How does the young-earth view of history explain this upward trend of conventional ages in the earth's rock layers? The concept of accelerated nuclear decay provides a compelling answer. Consider a burst of nuclear decay, corresponding to several billions of years' worth of decay at present rates. This occurs during the early part of the week of creation as the earth's original rocks are being formed. This affects the radioisotopes within the entire earth, including lower rocks which today are called *basement rock*. As a result, the original surface layer of the earth contains a large quantity of radioisotope daughter products. To a person with conventional assumptions of deep time, these decay products appear to imply an ancient age.

RATE research further indicates that an additional accelerated decay episode then took place during the Genesis flood event which occurred about 1,500 years after the creation. This episode corresponded to roughly 500 million years' worth of nuclear decay at today's rates. The Flood involved a period of intense geologic change on a global scale. Flood sediments, in some cases several miles in total thickness, were deposited during the year-long Flood. These sedimentary deposits generally cannot be directly dated by radioisotope methods. Instead, the ages are determined by magma which intrudes these sedimentary strata. It appears that volcanic rocks which intruded the lower layers contain more decay products than the volcanic rocks that intruded the upper layers. Thus, radioisotope dating methods generally give Paleozoic rocks older dates than rocks from the Mesozoic part of the record. The shallower strata represent sediments deposited later in the Flood. Their associated igneous intrusions have smaller amounts of decay products and hence yield younger ages. It appears that the radioisotopes in these rocks experienced a shorter period of accelerated nuclear decay. These results imply that accelerated decay likely persisted throughout the year of the Flood.

The inheritance and missing processes described in this chapter also operated during the Flood cataclysm, but probably played a secondary role in producing the pattern of radioisotope levels we measure in rocks. The RATE research concludes that the primary explanation for the large amount of daughter products now present in the earth's rocks are two periods of highly accelerated nuclear decay, with about 90 percent of the total occurring during the early part of creation week and the remainder during the year of the Genesis flood. The details, of course, need to be fleshed out with further research and study. It is a bold endeavor, to be sure, to account for the alleged 4.56 billion years of conventional earth history in a span of about 6,000 years. Our brief discussion, however, shows that there is a serious alternative explanation for the geologic record and the physical history of our world.

SUMMARY OF DISCORDANCE

Ten distinct rock units were explored by radioisotope analysis. The isotopes dated include potassium-argon, rubidium-strontium, samarium-neodymium, and lead-lead. The results show discordant ages due to contributions from at least three major sources. First, isotopes are known to be inherited to some degree from the earth's mantle which is the source material for basaltic rocks. Therefore, some portion of nuclear decay inferred for basaltic rocks actually occurred in their source material. The initial condition of the basaltic rocks thus remains unknown. Second, the fact of crustal exchange or mixing with the rising magmas has been widely documented. Radioisotope dating of many rocks therefore includes some contribution of nuclear decay from the rocks themselves, and also from their near neighbors. This means that rocks are open systems to some degree and that they are not accurate clocks. Third, consistent trends in the dating results for alpha and beta decays indicate that nuclear half-lives have not always remained constant. The RATE research causes us to conclude that this latter effect dominates the effects of the first two.

Three basic requirements were listed earlier as keys to the correct dating of rocks. These include known initial conditions for the rock, a closed system, and a constant rate of nuclear decay. It appears that all three of these dating essentials commonly fail at some level. Radioisotope data for rocks provide a wealth of information including their relative ages and possible interactions with their environment. However, absolute ages of rocks are not included in this information.

Chapter 9

THEORIES OF ACCELERATED NUCLEAR DECAY

Research by Eugene Chaffin

A CHALLENGE TO CONVENTIONAL SCIENCE

Over an eight-year period, the RATE team explored many aspects of radioisotope dating and the age of the earth. One fundamental conclusion is that radioactive half-lives have not remained constant throughout the earth's history. In particular, RATE research indicates nuclear decay was temporarily accelerated or speeded up on more than one occasion in the past. These suggested occasions are early during the creation week and also during the year of the Genesis flood. The evidence for accelerated decay comes from several directions as described in previous chapters.

While we believe the earth is young based on clear biblical data, many rocks contain an abundance of daughter atoms which give the appearance of being the product of nuclear decay. Is there strong evidence that these atoms indeed are the result of decay? The answer is *yes*, and for several reasons. The daughter atoms often are found in close proximity to sites where a significant portion of their radioactive parent atoms still resides. Also, radiohalos and fission tracks are found in great numbers. These are microscopic regions of damage within rocks which result from the nuclear decay process.

Accelerated decay would cause a rapid accumulation of the observed daughter atoms, radiohalos, and fission tracks. Additional evidence in favor of accelerated decay involves the zircon crystals described in chapter 4. Zircons show an accumulation of significant amounts of helium, one of the primary decay products of uranium. The diffusion rate of helium in zircon, as measured by RATE research, shows that the observed levels of helium in zircon cannot be maintained for more than a few thousand years. The clear implication is that the production of this helium by nuclear decay, some 1.5 billion years' worth at present decay rates, must have occurred recently, within the last few thousand years.

Accelerated decay requires radioactive half-lives to be temporarily shortened. If the earth's age truly is only thousands of years instead of multi-billions, then nuclear decay was greatly increased, in some cases a billion-fold or more. This proposal is a significant challenge to the physics and geology communities, which assume unchanging constants in nature. Nuclear half-lives are assumed to be very stable, as indeed they appear to be today. It is in the past that we suspect alteration took place. The RATE team fully realizes the implications of this challenge to current scientific thinking. A large-scale change in radioactive decay mechanisms in recent history represents an entirely new paradigm or approach to our thinking about nature. This new direction is part of the young-earth model which seriously questions the long-age, deep time assumptions of modern science.

Some critics have argued that the young-earth viewpoint is a hindrance to scientific progress. They claim that belief in biblical creation returns us to the dark ages of naïve, pre-scientific, and false views of natural history. However, such claims are mistaken. The questioning of radioisotope dating and the geologic time scale neither stifles inquiry nor hinders scientific progress. Instead, it serves the healthy purpose of uncovering assumptions and bias. The reappraisal of earth history also opens up entirely new areas for study and research as the RATE project has shown.

THE SHELTERED NUCLEUS

Radioactive decay involves the major alteration of an atom's nucleus or center core. Like the seed inside a peach, only on a vastly smaller scale, the nucleus is very well-shielded from the outside world. Many experiments have been conducted over the years in an attempt to modify nuclear half-lives. The goal of much of this effort is to find a way to rapidly neutralize radioactive waste materials. Radioactive atoms have been subjected to extremes of pressure, temperature, chemical alteration, magnetism, and electric fields. The results show very little change in half-lives, usually a few percent or less. There are occasional reports of much larger induced half-life changes. For example, German scientists have succeeded in stripping away all 187 electrons from radioactive atoms of rhenium-187 (Kerr, 1999). This directly exposed the rhenium nucleus to its chemical surroundings. As a result, the measured half-life for rhenium-187 decay dropped from 42 billion years to just 33 years. This extreme alteration of rhenium atoms is a special, isolated case. Such conditions might possibly occur within the hot core of a star but certainly not under any earth-like conditions.

The challenge remains to explain how accelerated decay on a large scale could possibly occur in the earth. The original creation from nothing, or *ex nihilo* in Latin, was clearly supernatural. Likewise, the theological reasons for accelerated decay and the mechanisms behind it may lie entirely beyond the limits of scientific inquiry. Still, it is of interest to apply our present knowledge of the nucleus to explore possible mechanisms for accelerated decay. The results provide a few, preliminary hints of how half-lives may have been altered in the past.

THE NUCLEAR POTENTIAL WELL

One possible way to change decay rates applies specifically to the alpha decay process. As Table 2-1 shows, alpha decay occurs for the radioisotopes samarium-147, thorium-232, uranium-235, and uranium-238. For these isotopes, the decaying nucleus emits an alpha particle at high speed. The nucleus itself consists of many protons and neutrons which are held together tightly by the nuclear force. This force, while essential to the stability of all matter, is not well understood. It acts over a very short distance to provide the strong attraction between the nuclear particles. In the case of uranium-238, for example, the nucleus holds 92 protons and 146 neutrons, all tightly bound together in a dense cluster. During radioactive decay the alpha particle must form and then somehow break loose and escape the extreme nuclear binding force exerted by the remaining cluster of protons and neutrons.

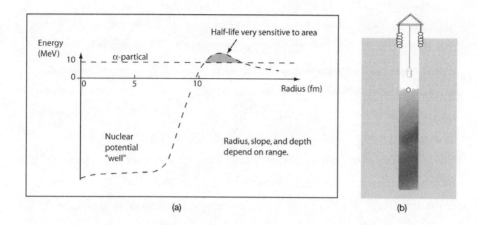

Figure 9-1. Part (a) shows a potential well which represents the nucleus of an atom. Energy is measured in the vertical direction in millions of electron volts, or MeV. The steep dotted line shows the size of the nucleus with a radius of about ten fermi (fm, 10^{-15} meters). Alpha particles are trapped inside the well and may escape to the right. Part (b) shows a ball floating within a well. The escape of an alpha particle from the nucleus is analogous to the ball escaping from the well.

Figure 9-1(a) pictures a nucleus as a potential well, a model often used in physics studies. The vertical direction represents increasing energy, measured in units called millions of *electron volts*, or MeV. The horizontal axis measures distance outward from the center of the nucleus. The near-vertical dotted line represents the outer boundary of the nucleus. The nuclear particles are held captive inside this potential well. The upper horizontal dotted line represents the energy level an alpha particle might have within the nucleus. The upper shaded peak at the top right side of the well is called the *Coulomb barrier* which confines the alpha particle. In nuclear alpha decay, the particle must pass through this barrier to gain its freedom from the nucleus. This is a fascinating process called *quantum mechanical tunneling* which does not seem physically possible. The alpha particle is trapped inside the well, yet it somehow escapes. It is almost as if an object were to move directly through a solid wall. Yet there is a small, finite probability that the alpha particle can escape the potential well which holds it, and indeed this happens regularly. For comparison, Figure 9-1(b) shows a water well with a floating ball inside. Alpha decay is equivalent to the ball somehow passing directly through the upper wall of the water well and rolling away. Of course, the nuclear well is ten thousand trillion times smaller (10^{16}) than a water well. The quantum effects that we observe, including the tunneling process, are limited to the very small scale of nature. The ball will only escape the water well with outside help!

It is known that the alpha decay process is very sensitive to the depth and radius of the nuclear potential well. For this reason, nuclei which decay by alpha emission have a vast range of half-lives, extending from microseconds to trillions of years. The range is more than 23 orders of magnitude, or one followed by 23 zeros. This is an example of an unusually large range for a measured physical quantity, similar to the atomic diffusion values discussed in chapter 4 and plotted in Figure 4-6.

The RATE research team explored the alpha decay process by making theoretical calculations of the change in nuclear half-life as the potential well depth was varied. It was found that a ten percent decrease in well depth results in a decrease in nuclear half-life by as much as 100 million. Another way to express this idea of a shallower well is that the nuclear force was weakened. The result was a decrease in the half-life. Moreover, a ten percent increase in the energy of the alpha particle decreased the nuclear half-life by 100,000 times. Such an energy alteration brings the alpha particle closer to the top of its potential well. This makes it much easier for the alpha particle to tunnel outward. However, any historical increase in alpha particle energy by more than ten percent seems to be precluded by the near-constancy of radiohalo radii through time. A change in the potential well depth or alpha particle energy may be on the right track in explaining how rapid

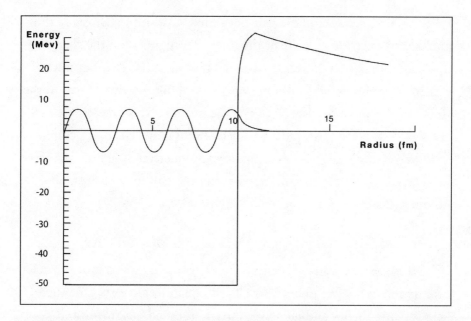

Figure 9-2. Illustration of a standing wave inside the potential well of a nucleus. An alpha particle can be represented by such a wave. Notice how the right end of the wave dies out beyond the right edge of the nucleus. Theoretical adjustments of the alpha particle's energy and the shape of the well are found to dramatically change the decay time of the radioactive nucleus.

decay occurred in the past. As usual, however, more theoretical study is needed.

There is another intriguing connection between quantum mechanics and nuclear alpha decay. Similar to light, an alpha particle displays a dual nature or behavior. That is, it displays properties of both a particle located in one position, and also a wave which spreads out and becomes non-localized. Thus, it is possible to picture an alpha particle existing inside the nucleus as a "standing wave," similar to the vibration of a violin string. Figure 9-2 shows a nuclear potential well with a standing wave positioned inside. A portion of the alpha wave may extend into or beyond the Coulomb barrier. In effect, this means that the alpha particle has a small probability of existing outside the nucleus. Theoretical

RATE analysis explored how half-life varied with small changes in the nuclear radius, the curvature of the nuclear well wall, and the shape of the Coulomb barrier. Several additional modifications of other nuclear variables are also possible. The results show significant differences in the ability of the alpha particle to escape the nucleus. This type of research involves complex mathematical modeling of the nucleus using computer software. The value of these studies is in understanding how changes in the various nuclear parameters can alter the half-lives of unstable isotopes.

STRING THEORY AND NUCLEAR DECAY

Other current fields of scientific research include even more abstract concepts than nuclear potential wells and quantum theory. One such field is string theory and its newer variations called *superstring* and *m-theories*. These are mathematical attempts to describe the building blocks of matter on the smallest possible scale. String theory suggests that all matter consists of vibrating loops of energy which are trillions of times smaller than atoms, electrons, and other elementary particles. One might imagine an energized rubber band with its sides rapidly moving inward and outward. However, the theoretical strings are nothing like rubber bands, thread, or yarn. Instead they are tiny kinks or knots in the fabric of space-time which involve several more dimensions than we are aware of. As many as ten dimensions have been proposed. These ideas go far beyond any physical picture, because we are only familiar with the four everyday dimensions of length, height, width, and time.

String theory is of special interest because its accompanying mathematics is both elegant and consistent. This is always found to be the case when mathematics correctly describes parts of the physical universe. The mathematics of string theory also has the potential to unify the distinct forces in nature, including a quantum theory of gravity. This long-sought unification would bring together several concepts of physics into one explanation, theory, or equation. String theory may or may not be the key to this deeper understanding of creation. So far, there is no direct experimental evidence to validate string theory. Nevertheless, hundreds of physicists and mathematicians are investigating its possible ability to describe our world. One might say that mathematics is the very language of creation. While this precise language is elegant and insightful, it also can be exceedingly complex.

The RATE team has considered whether an application of string theory might be useful in identifying the mechanisms behind accelerated isotope decay. The extra space dimensions, if they indeed exist, are not accessible to our everyday world. They are said to be compactified or confined to an incredibly small size. That is, they are tightly curled up into "manifolds" and they remain entirely invisible to our everyday world. String theory shows a direct connection between the size or radius of these hidden dimensions and a particular constant of nature called the *fermi* constant. This is an important number because the rate of nuclear beta decay is very sensitive to the fermi constant. Beta decay involves such radioisotopes as carbon-14, potassium-40, rubidium-87, lutetium-176, and rhenium-187 (Table 2-1).

If string theory turns out to be a correct description of nature, then we may have a mathematical model that could account for an acceleration of the beta form of nuclear decay. For example, such a model could explore small, temporary adjustments of unseen dimensions, perhaps by the direct hand of the Creator. This might alter the fermi constant and in turn, adjust nuclear decay rates significantly. There are several "ifs" in this exploration of accelerated decay and it is presented here only as an example of ongoing research. String theory is highly abstract to be sure, but it has opened up many new avenues of research. This discussion shows how little we actually know about the fundamental nature of matter on the smallest scale. The rest of this chapter summarizes the RATE team's view of accelerated nuclear decay.

THE EPISODES OF ACCELERATED DECAY

The RATE effort has gathered evidence for multiple episodes of accelerated decay within the past few thousand years. Two or more distinct times in history may be involved, each with a clear theological connection. The initial possibility covers the first two days of the creation week, before any life was present on earth. After all, accelerated decay unleashes a lethal spray of radiation which appears to limit such an event to the pre-life or *pre-biotic* days of creation. Vegetation was created on day 3 and animals appeared on days 5 and 6. Our first parents, Adam and Eve, arrived on the sixth day.

The Precambrian rocks of the earth are largely without fossils. This suggests that much Precambrian rock represents the original created crust of the earth. As Table 3-1 shows, the Precambrian record encompasses some 88 percent of the conventional time-line of earth history, or about 4 billion years. The RATE team concludes that an acceleration of nuclear decay on a great scale took place during the creation week as these rocks were put in place. That is, several billion years worth of decay took place in just days.

Some might object that nuclear decay ought logically to be a result of the Curse, or the Fall of mankind, as described in Genesis 3. If so, then nuclear decay could exist only after this point in history. However, nuclear activity cannot automatically be ruled out during the time prior to the Curse. Indeed, there is no obvious connection between the Curse and nuclear processes. Ever since the fourth day of creation, for example, the sun and other stars have apparently been heated, at least partially, by complex nuclear fusion reactions with the emission of radiation.

The Bible indicates that many degenerative physical processes began at the Fall, including the growth of thorns and thistles, the crawling nature of serpents, pain in childbirth, and ultimately, death itself. It is conceivable that nuclear decay also may have been temporarily adjusted during this time of major reprogramming of nature. If so, there would be the requirement to providentially protect living things from a massive amount of resulting radiation. The present consensus of the RATE team is that there is no compelling evidence for such a pulse of decay at this point in earth history.

On the other hand, there is abundant evidence for a significant episode of accelerated decay during the Genesis flood event. The Flood included an unprecedented period of global tectonics, erosion, and rapid rock-forming processes. The rocks resulting from this catastrophic event give clear evidence of nuclear decay with resulting daughter products, radiohalos, and fission tracks. The vast majority of the rock strata above the Precambrian level are considered by many creationists to represent Flood deposits. In the conventional time scale, the Paleozoic and Mesozoic eras alone span more than four hundred million years. The RATE research concludes that accelerated decay on this scale occurred during the single year of the Flood. There is the obvious issue of protecting the precious animal and human life on board the ark. The water barrier between the ark and the earth's rock layers could have played a major role along with divine intervention.

Many recent, post-Flood rock formations also hold a record of substantial nuclear decay. This again implies decay rates somewhat shorter than those presently observed. This suggests that during the immediate post-Flood period there was a "tapering off" of accelerated decay to the half-life values which we measure today. In summary, there are three time periods when the acceleration of nuclear decay likely occurred: creation, Flood, and immediate post-Flood times. We conclude the vast majority occurred during the early part of the creation week and during the Genesis flood.

FURTHER QUESTIONS TO PONDER

The RATE team proposes two main episodes of accelerated nuclear decay occurring over a time scale of just a few thousand years. This idea raises a number of interesting questions.

Purpose of Acceleration

Why was nuclear decay accelerated in the first place, and what purpose or function did it serve? A temporary alteration of nuclear constants obviously lies within the Creator's realm of activity. It is clear that the One who created all things can alter physical constants and laws at His will. In fact, most biblical miracles require a temporary suspension of basic natural laws.

Heat Dissipation

The heat energy given off during nuclear decay raises an important question. What prevented the earth from melting completely during the rapid decay which amounted to millions of year's worth at present rates? Calculations show that this much decay of uranium and thorium atoms within a typical rock mass would raise the rock temperature as high as 22,000°C. This temperature is nearly four times hotter than the surface of the sun and would likely vaporize entire rock masses in explosive events, but the crust of the earth did not melt during the Flood period. In fact, the presence of radiohalos and fission tracks in many rocks shows that rock temperatures remained below about 150°C during the formation of the halos and tracks. Otherwise, these crystal defects would be thermally erased. Also, zircons in many rocks still contain helium atoms resulting from accelerated decay, yet the zircon crystals themselves were not melted during the nuclear decay process.

Somehow the enormous amount of heat resulting from isotope decay must have dissipated quickly. One tentative, rather novel proposal is called *cosmological cooling* (Humphreys, 2000). It is highly theoretical in nature and involves general relativity, higher dimensions, and a rapid expansion of space. Consider a kitchen refrigerator which is cooled by the expansion of a confined, compressed gas. In somewhat analogous fashion, an expansion of space would result in cooling on a universal scale. In this explanation, the heat energy generated by accelerated nuclear decay goes into the expansion of the fabric of space itself. The key is to have accelerated decay simultaneously accompanied by a temporary, large-scale stretching of the space surrounding earth. Since there is evidence of much radioactive decay throughout the solar system and in space beyond, the expansion must be universal in its extent. There are definite hints in Scripture of an expansion of space during the creation week and also during the Genesis flood (Humphreys, 2000). It is proposed that an enormous expansion of space, 20-fold times or greater, occurred during the Flood event.

Big-bang enthusiasts also propose an inflationary stretching of space. However, their inflationary big bang occurs at the very beginning of time, within the first second, and only increases the universe from atom size to that of approximately a marble. In contrast, the cosmological cooling model places its expansion in the time frame of the Flood. Such an extreme alteration of the physical universe actually might drop the temperature too far and cause the reverse problem of over-heating, that is, a frozen earth. Further theoretical work is ongoing regarding the amount of heat produced by nuclear decay and the possible mechanisms for its removal. The RATE team views the extreme heat generation associated with accelerated decay as a serious issue, but not an insurmountable problem.

RADIATION HAZARD

Radiation that accompanies rapid nuclear decay is of immediate concern to creatures living on the earth at the time of its occurrence. This includes Noah and his family during the Flood event. The barrier of flood waters may have provided a measure of protection from underground radiation. However, the decay of potassium-40 presents another peril. Potassium is the seventh most abundant element in our bodies, comprising about 0.4 percent of our weight. This may sound like a minor component, but it totals about 10^{25} potassium atoms, or ten-trillion-trillion atoms. Potassium plays an important role in many chemical processes in living cells. Natural potassium consists of about 0.0118 percent radioactive potassium-40. The current half-life of this isotope is about 1.25 billion years. If this value was greatly reduced by accelerated decay, lethal internal radiation poisoning and heating could well result. Therefore, the suggestion arises that living creatures in the past, including people, may not have incorporated significant amounts of the particular isotope potassium-40 into their bodies. This possibility is a topic of current research.

Carbon-14 is another radioisotope which exists in trace amounts inside our bodies. An average adult carries about ten kilograms (22 pounds) of carbon. This is mostly carbon-12 with only about one part-per-trillion of carbon-14. Within an adult body, the internal carbon-14 decays at a rate of about seven million carbon-14 decays per hour. This level of radiation is actually very low (about 50 nanocuries) and is entirely harmless, but what about accelerated decay? As with potassium-40, a rapid decay of internal carbon-14 could be very unhealthy. However, as discussed in chapter 3, the significant levels of carbon-14 still found in coal and other fossil material indicate the amount of accelerated decay of carbon-14 was relatively modest. Moreover, the carbon-14 in the pre-Flood world was diluted with at least 100 times more carbon-12 than at present. Therefore, the total amount of carbon-14 in a given organism at the time of the Flood was likely at least 100 times less than is the case today. Therefore, it appears the decay of carbon-14 within organisms during the Flood was much less a potential problem when compared with potassium-40.

The exploration of accelerated nuclear decay mechanisms has taken us to many unexpected topics. These include the strong force holding the nucleus together, the quantum tunneling of alpha particles out of the nucleus, cosmic strings, higher dimensions, and radioactive potassium-40 and carbon-14 inside living creatures. Such is the nature of scientific research, where insights often come from surprising directions.

Chapter 10

A PROPER READING

OF GENESIS 1:1–2:3

Research by Steven Boyd

THE GENESIS ACCOUNT OF CREATION

Each member of the RATE team holds to a high view of Scripture. This means that we regard the Bible as a uniquely inspired book given to mankind by the Creator. The original Hebrew, Aramaic, and Greek text of Scripture includes a rich variety of literature. These forms include historical narrative, poetry, law, apocalyptic writings, and letters. Of special interest to the study of earth history is the proper interpretation of the Genesis creation account. The details of creation are recorded in the 34 verses of Genesis 1:1–2:3. Over the years there has been much discussion and debate over the meaning of this passage, and three distinct views have surfaced. First, some readers of Genesis assume that the book is an outdated, pre-scientific document which is riddled with errors and is simply wrong. Genesis is said to be just one of many mythical stories from the distant past. Clearly, this view does not recognize Scripture as uniquely inspired by the Creator. In the second approach to Genesis, the creation passage is seen as a form of poetry which should not be read as literal history. It is said to convey a sense of truth about origins, but it is not a literal description of actual events. The days of creation may represent long geologic periods in deep time. That is, the biblical creation week is a figurative expression for gradual changes which occurred on the earth, perhaps millions or billions of years ago.

The third view takes the creation account as literal narrative history. The RATE group firmly holds to this third position, regarding Genesis 1:1–2:3 as a literal description of how the world and the universe began. The Book of Genesis describes the supernatural, literal creation week with 24-hour days. Certainly God could have created the physical universe in just six microseconds, or in contrast, over a span of trillions of years. It is clear, however, that the six-day period is a pattern established for the benefit of humanity. In fact, these six days, plus the day of rest, give rise to our calendar system with its seven-day week.

One important aspect of RATE research is a thorough investigation of the proper meaning of the Genesis creation passage. We did not dwell on the first approach which assumes there are errors in Scripture. After all, the Bible has successfully withstood every challenge and historical test. However, it is the second, non-literal approach to Genesis which needs to be evaluated. This is the view of those who attempt to read an ancient earth history into the biblical text. The approach is somewhat inviting because the alternative, the young-earth creation view, conflicts directly with the well-established conventions of modern science. However, the important question remains, whether it is legitimate to read the Genesis account as non-literal, poetic literature.

NARRATIVE AND POETRY DEFINED

How does one determine whether a text is a narrative or poetry? Narratives are defined as telling a factual story, with three general elements. The first element is the setting which gives the time, place, and circumstances of the unfolding story. The second element includes the set of characters that are part of the story. The third element is the sequence of events that comprise the story plot.

Biblical Hebrew poetry also has several defining features which help identify it. First, some of the oldest available manuscripts have passages which are organized and labeled as verse. Examples include the Balaam Oracles (Num. 23), the Song of Deborah and Barak (Judg. 5), the Song of David (2 Sam. 22), Psalm 119, and Psalm 136. A second trait of poetry is its distinct style. Hebrew poetry does not necessarily possess meter or rhyme. It often includes similar sounds and arrangements of words, parallelism of thoughts (Prov. 30:18–19), symmetry, balance, and brevity. Poems are highly structured literature which offers profound ideas. A third distinction of poetry is its goal to engage the reader's five senses and emotions. The poet wants the reader to hear, see, smell, taste, and feel the experience.

As helpful as these descriptions are, the nature of poetry and narrative is still debated. To correctly classify a text such as Genesis 1:1–2:3, a rigorous analysis is needed. One such approach is a statistical analysis of biblical Hebrew verbs.

HEBREW VERB FORMS

By application of the preceding criteria for narratives and poetry, it is possible to categorize biblical texts. The RATE study surveyed the distinct choice of language used for historical narratives and poetry passages throughout the Old Testament. Both of these literature styles, also called *genres*, are common in Scripture. The RATE goal was to determine which category best fits the passage Genesis 1:1–2:3. The particular language feature chosen for this study was the relative distribution of finite verbs. The finite verbs are those defined as having different forms or inflections for person (I, you, he, they), gender (masculine, feminine), and number (singular, plural). There are four finite verb forms in biblical Hebrew. These are given the names *preterite, imperfect, perfect,* and *waw-perfect.* Each describes a particular type of action. Table 10-1 summarizes the meanings of these four verb forms with Hebrew and English examples. The finite verbs in Scripture are well suited for technical analysis. Because they are a countable feature, statistical methods can be applied. Also, finite verbs are at the heart of any text because they reflect the main action of the character(s) or their movement through time.

PAIRED SCRIPTURE TEXTS

Biblical authors wrote texts under the inspiration of the Holy Spirit according to 2 Timothy 3:16 and 2 Peter 1:19–21. The language they chose, including the verbs, shaped the intended meaning. Whether an author wanted the text to be treated as poetry or narrative was evident to the original readers. Today, it is possible to determine this intended meaning by a careful study of its linguistic features.

Table 10-1. A summary of the finite verb forms used in biblical Hebrew. The comment column summarizes the general verb usage. Phrases with English and Hebrew examples are included on the right side.

Verb Form	Comment	English Example (swim)	Hebrew Example
Preterite	Comes first in a sentence. Describes a past action, state, or condition.	She swam.	Abraham *kept* my commandments (Gen. 26:5).
Imperfect	Normally used for present/future/ general present.	She is swimming/ will swim/swims.	The lips of the priest *keep* knowledge (Mal. 2:7).
	A habitual action in the past.	She would swim (daily).	If the owner never *kept* his bull penned . . . (Exod. 21:29).
	Modally, expressing the mood of the verb.	She must/should swim.	You *must keep* my covenant (Gen. 17:9).
Perfect	Normally used for a single event in the past/anterior past which is being contrasted to the main action.	She swam/had swam.	His father *kept* the matter in mind (Gen. 37:11).
Waw-perfect	Comes first in a clause. Is used for repeated or habitual action in the past.	She would/used to swim.	The pillar of cloud *would stand* at the opening of the tent and would speak with Moses (Exod. 33:9).
	Continues the force of the previous verb (pv) in the future.		
	If pv indicates future	(She will run) and swim.	They *will keep* food in the cities (Gen. 41:35).
	If pv is an imperative	(Run) and swim.	*Take* (imperative) for yourselves wagons from the land of Egypt for your little ones and your wives and *carry* your father and come (Gen. 45:19).

Several historical events in the Old Testament are written in both the narrative and poetic styles of literature. These are called *paired texts* and they provide an excellent opportunity for the comparison of verb use. Two examples follow.

Story	Narrative Form	Poetic Form
The Children of Israel cross over the Red Sea	Exodus 14	Exodus 15:1–19 Song of Moses
Barak and Deborah defeat the Canaanites	Judges 4	Judges 5 Song of Deborah and Barak

The distribution of finite verbs in these paired passages is shown on the left side of the bar graph in Figure 10-1. The heights of the bars measure the fraction of verbs that are in each of the four forms listed above. It is clear that the use of the preterite verb form dominates the narrative stories. These preterite verbs indicate a flow of events during a specific time sequence. In contrast, the imperfect and perfect verbs are more common in the poetic texts. The fourth Hebrew verb form, the *waw*-perfect, does not often appear in any of the passages shown in Figure 10-1. You may notice that the four decimal fractions for a particular text in Figure 10-1 do not add up to unity or one. The reason is that the texts also include additional non-finite forms which were part of the total verb count.

For comparison, Figure 10-1 also shows the verb occurrence for four additional Old Testament passages. Toward the center of the figure is the verb distribution for Genesis 1:1–2-3, the main text under discussion in this chapter. The height of the bar for the preterite verb form shows that Genesis 1:1–2:3 closely fits the pattern of narrative structure. In contrast, Psalm 104 is a poetic account of creation with a majority of imperfect finite verbs. The Flood account, covering Genesis 6–9, adheres to the historical narrative pattern. One final passage, Psalm 105, gives a narrative history of Israel. In each of these cases there is a consistent pattern of preterite and imperfect verb usage.

SAMPLING AND VISUALIZATION OF TEXTS

Encouraged by the results with paired texts as summarized in Figure 10-1, a thorough analysis of finite verbs in Scripture was conducted. A survey of the entire Old Testament identified 295 narrative and 227 poetic texts for a total of 522 distinct texts. The computer software program called *BibleWorks* was employed to search the Westminster Theological Morphological database. This valuable database gives a complete grammatical analysis of every word in the

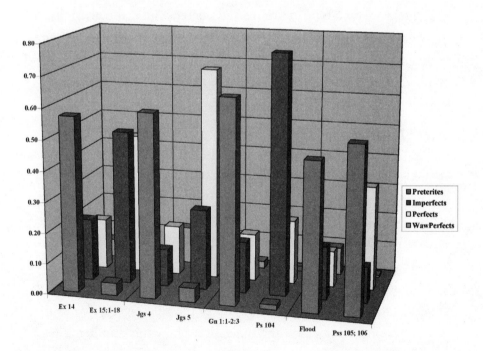

Figure 10-1. A bar graph showing finite verb usage for eight biblical texts. The height of the bars shows the frequency of use of four finite verb forms. Narrative texts use more preterite verbs while poetic texts use more perfects and imperfect verbs.

Hebrew Bible. Hebrew verbs have several parts, including root, stem, person, gender, and number. Altogether, a total of some 9,903 verbs were counted and categorized in the 522 texts. Of these total verbs, 2,099 were identified as the finite variety. Since this wealth of data was impractical for analysis, random sampling was applied. This required care because finite verb distributions may vary with the Old Testament time period, the verb usage by particular authors, and other factors.

We wanted to be certain that all three major divisions of the Hebrew Bible were represented in the verb analysis. The first five Old Testament books are called the Pentateuch, the Law, or Torah. The second division includes the Prophets with 21 books, further subdivided into the Former Prophets and Latter Prophets. The third major division includes the Writings with 13 books. Table 10-2 lists several texts of each type, narrative and poetry, within the divisions. A "stratified" random sample of 97 texts was chosen across the categories so that all were represented in the sample. This totaled 48 narrative and 49 poetic texts. The finite verb counts were tallied for these selected texts.

Bar graphs for the analyzed texts have an appearance very similar to Figure 10-1. That is, there is a consistent division between finite verb usage in the narrative and poetic texts. Another device used to visualize the results is the scatter plot. Figure 10-2 shows side-by-side scatter plots which summarize the sampled narrative and poetic texts. The vertical axis measures the ratio of preterite verbs to all four kinds of finite verbs. Narrative passages are represented by diamonds on the left side of Figure 10-2. Notice that the median or middle value for the preterite ratio is 0.52. That is, the verbs in these passages were of the preterite form 52 percent of the time. To see how this number arises, consider the narrative passage Genesis 31, the story of Laban. This text has 70 preterite verbs out of a total of 153 finite verbs. Therefore, its ratio of preterites to total finite verbs is 70/153 = 0.458.

Table 10-2. Examples of poetic and narrative Scripture passages which were included in the Old Testament sample. Altogether, 97 texts were tested statistically for their finite verb distribution.

Narrative	Poetry
Story of Joseph Genesis 37–50	Jacob blesses his sons Genesis 49
Joshua's conquest of the Promised Land Joshua 1–10	Song of Moses Exodus 15
Samson's life Judges 13–16	Oracles of Balaam Numbers 23–24
Books of Ruth, Esther, and Nehemiah	Song of Moses Deuteronomy 32
Court history of David 2 Samuel 11–20	Song of Deborah Judges 5
Account of Jehoiakim Jeremiah 36	Ministry of Elijah Prayer of Hannah 1 Samuel 2:1-10
Defeat of Jerusalem by Babylon 2 Kings 25	Song of David 2 Samuel 22
Books of 1 and 2 Kings and 1 and 2 Chronicles	Books of Isaiah, Psalms, and Proverbs
	Books of Job, Lamentations, and the Minor Prophets

If there was no preference for particular verbs in biblical passages, then one would expect all the data to fall on the same horizontal line with a ratio of ¼ = 0.25. Instead, however, the narrative texts show a pronounced higher number of preterite verbs. The highest diamond on the left side of the figure has a preterite verb ratio of 0.81. This is the

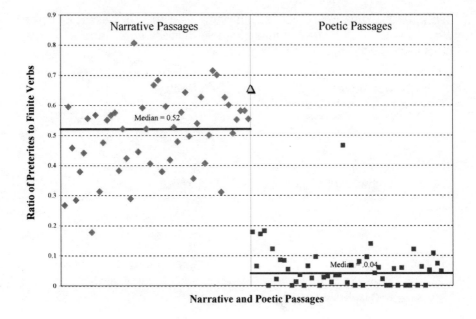

Figure 10-2. Side-by-side scatter plots of preterite verb usage for narrative (diamonds on the left) and poetic (squares on the right) passages. The vertical axis measures the ratio of preterite verbs to all four finite verb types. Notice the predominance of preterite verb usage for narrative texts, and less preterite usage for poetic texts.

passage Judges 3:8–31 in which preterite verbs comprise 81 percent of the total finite verbs used.

The squares on the right side of Figure 10-2 represent the poetic passages. For poetry, the median preterite ratio is 0.04. Let us apply the poetic passage Deuteronomy 32 to Figure 10-2. This poem or song was recited by Moses to the Israelites. The text has 20 preterite verbs out of a total of 117 finite verbs. The ratio this time is 20/117 = 0.171. The scatter plot shows that many of the poetic texts have a similar or smaller ratio. In fact, some of the poetic passages have a zero percent occurrence of the preterite verb form.

Of the 97 texts sampled, only two are clearly misclassified. Verb usage places the non-poetic passage Exodus 33 in the poetry category.

THOUSANDS . . . NOT BILLIONS

It is shown by the lowest diamond on the left side of Figure 10-2. This passage has an unusual structure with more *waw*-perfect verbs than preterites. The reason for this is that a large number of future tenses occur in the verses. The second misclassified reference is Ezekiel 19. Verb usage places it in the narrative category; however, this chapter describes kings of Judah with highly figurative language. It is shown by the highest square on the right side of Figure 10-2. Actually, Ezekiel 19 is neither narrative nor poetry, but instead is in a specialized category called *apocalyptic*.

Note the triangle in the center of Figure 10-2. This shows the preterite verb ratio for the passage in question, Genesis 1:1–2:3. Clearly, the creation account falls in the narrative category.

APPLICATION OF STATISTICS

A statistical technique called *logistic regression* was next applied to the 97 selected texts. Logistic regression is useful in making predictions when there are just two choices involved. In our case, the technique predicts the probability that an unknown text is a narrative, given its distribution of preterites. There are a number of mathematical formulas required which are explained in the technical RATE volumes. The result is shown in Figure 10-3. The vertical axis on the left measures the probability of an Old Testament passage being a narrative. The value is zero for poetry and one for narrative. From the ratios of preterites to total finite verbs for all the passages considered, the curved line was calculated. Passages with a small preterite verb ratio, left of the vertical dotted line, have a high probability of being poetry. Passages falling to the right of the vertical dotted line are likely narrative. The key passage under consideration, Genesis 1:1–2:3, is represented by the triangle shown on the far right side of Figure 10-3. The mathematics of logistic regression allows a calculation of the probability that this creation passage is narrative rather than poetry. The result is that Genesis 1:1–2:3 is statistically

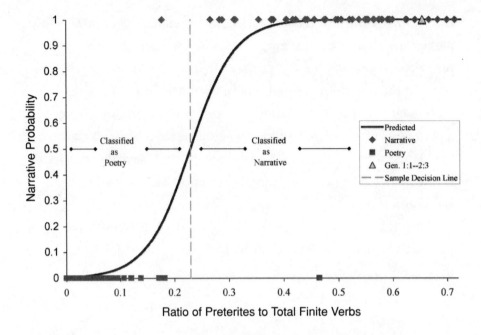

Figure 10-3. The solid curved line is called a logistic regression curve. The vertical axis measures the probability that an Old Testament passage is narrative, based on the use of preterite verbs. The probability is zero for poetry and unity or one for narrative. Passages with high preterite verb counts, falling to the right of the vertical dotted line, are likely narrative. The triangle on the upper right represents Genesis 1:1–2:3, which is clearly literal, narrative history.

classified as narrative with a probability of 0.9999. This value, virtually one, shows an extraordinary level of confidence. The biblical creation account clearly is not poetry but instead is a literal description in real time of supernatural events.

HISTORICAL FICTION VERSUS NONFICTION

The RATE research shows that the Genesis creation account is clearly written as narrative literature. However, critics may still claim that Genesis and the rest of the Old Testament contain non-literal stories of history. To counter this challenge, consider three distinct features of Old Testament narratives in general. They verify that the biblical authors of narrative portrayed real historical events. The features are adapted from the book by Meir Sternberg (1985).

1. Detailed genealogies are given. Adam's genealogy up through Noah is listed in Genesis 5. Genesis 11 then continues this genealogy from Noah to Abraham.

2. God's people are defined in terms of their past history. For example, Abraham is commanded to leave his home country and to launch a new nation (Gen. 12).

3. The past is often reviewed and summarized. Job 38–41 describes many details of the original and the present-day creation. Also, Jeremiah 2:1–13 examines God's dealings with Israel over time.

These important features of biblical narrative could be added to almost indefinitely. They are a reminder of the intricacy, integrity, and unity of the biblical text.

THE MEANING OF GENESIS 1:1–2:3

The distribution of finite verbs in Hebrew narrative writing differs distinctly from that used in poetry. Moreover, statistical analysis categorizes biblical texts as narrative or poetry to a high level of accuracy. Genesis 1:1–2:3 is determined to be narrative with a probability of virtually one. There follow at least three major implications from this study. First, it is not statistically defensible to interpret Genesis 1:1–2:3 as poetry or metaphor. Second, since Genesis 1:1–2:3 clearly is narrative, it should be read as other Hebrew narratives are intended to be read. That is, the creation account describes actual events which carry an unmistakable theological message. Third, when Genesis 1:1–2:3 is read as narrative, there is only one tenable view: God created everything during six literal days. This is surely the plain, direct intention of the text. Furthermore, the unchanging Scripture message has priority over all transient models of earth history. The RATE team concludes that Scripture is the standard to which interpretations of scientific data must conform. This does not imply the rejection of any data whatsoever. However, it does call for the positive channeling of data interpretation in a proper biblical direction.

Chapter 11

RATE
Conclusions

A Beginning

This book surveys eight years of radioisotope research by the team of RATE scientists. Since each member maintains a professional career, participation in the RATE project required an extra commitment of time. The effort included many hours of laboratory work, travel, data analysis, discussion, and writing. It also required a large financial investment and sincere appreciation is expressed to each donor. The title of this final chapter does not imply that our research on radioisotope dating and the age of the earth has concluded. Instead, it has just begun. Several new areas for scientific exploration were identified during the project. RATE scientists and colleagues will actively continue the evaluation of current radioisotope dating techniques. As is the general case in science, there is a need for additional research on nearly every topic in this book. On the positive side, however, the RATE project has made good progress in challenging evolution's icon or assumption of deep time. The following sections highlight the guiding principles of RATE, its major findings, and some of the unfinished work.

Guiding Principles of RATE

One principle agreed on by all the RATE members is that the earth is young, on the order of 6,000 years old. This is not simply a working hypothesis to be tested as to whether it is true or false. Instead, it is a basic conclusion drawn from the biblical record of creation as written by the only One who was present, God himself. This creation position is neither outdated nor anti-scientific. It does not require a stifling of scientific inquiry or the rejection of any data. Instead, the creation viewpoint presents entirely new directions for research and data interpretation. As just one example, the Bible describes in detail the flood of Noah's day, an event which completely transformed the earth's surface as well as human history. Flood geology on this global scale provides unique research opportunities which simply are not recognized by the current science establishment.

A second guiding principle the RATE team realized from the start is that a large amount of nuclear decay has taken place in the past. This history of radioactive decay is amply demonstrated by accumulated daughter decay products in close association with their parent isotopes in many earth materials. There are also vast numbers of defects caused by nuclear decay in crystalline rocks, including radiohalos and fission tracks. We assume that the earth was not created with an appearance of age at this microscopic level of detail. Alongside this principle, however, there is not the usual constraint that radioisotope decay has always been governed by today's measured nuclear half-life values. Instead, the RATE team concludes that there have been episodes of major acceleration of nuclear decay in the past. This intriguing concept is directly related to the biblical, catastrophic view of earth history.

RATE FINDINGS

Only the major results of the RATE effort will be summarized in this section. Some of the secondary findings, not covered here, may eventually turn out to be important keys to our understanding of radioisotope data. All the results, both major and minor, are included in the two technical RATE volumes. The following conclusions are listed in no particular order, and are taken from the preceding chapters.

1. For some years there has been a growing realization that carbon-14 atoms are found where they are not expected. With a half-life of 5,730 years, C-14 should no longer exist within "ancient" fossils, carbonate rocks, or coal. Yet small quantities of C-14 are indeed found in such samples on a worldwide scale. The RATE work extends this information with carbon-14 measurements in additional coal samples and also in diamonds. The RATE carbon-14 experiments on diamonds are the first ever reported in the literature. Measurable levels of C-14 are found in every case for both coal and diamond samples. This evidence supports a limited age for the earth. There is a widely held misconception that carbon-14 dating is in direct conflict with creation and the young-earth view. Instead, however, the carbon-14 findings strongly support a recent supernatural creation.

2. Zircons play a prominent part in the RATE studies. These are tiny crystals which often occur in granite, one of the most abundant rock types on earth. Within their crystal structures, many zircons hold helium atoms which result from the decay of internal uranium atoms. Zircons brought to the surface from deep underground are assumed to be ancient. The New Mexico zircons studied by the RATE team have a radioisotope age of 1.5 billion years. If this were true, then the internal helium atoms should long ago have escaped from the zircons. Instead, however, the RATE scientists and others find high concentrations of helium still present inside the zircon crystals.

RATE research obtained some of the first high-precision data on helium diffusion in zircon. A theoretical model based on this data gives an age for the earth of about 6,000 years. The presence of helium in zircons is a serious challenge to the concept of deep time. The helium also represents compelling evidence of accelerated nuclear decay in the past.

3. Radiohalos are tiny spherical defects in rocks. They result from the decay of clusters of radioactive atoms, mainly uranium and polonium. The frequent occurrence of these halos in rocks is evidence for widespread nuclear decay. Halos are present in abundance in granites whose formation accompanied the Genesis flood. This indicates that a large-scale acceleration of nuclear decay occurred during the year-long Flood event.

There is a longstanding mystery concerning radiohalos. Many of them appear to have formed during the decay of short-lived polonium radioisotopes. These transient isotopes must in turn be supplied by the decay of other isotopes with much longer half-lives. However, evidence for the long-life parents often is missing. These halo-forming

THOUSANDS ... NOT BILLIONS

isotopes include the polonium isotopes 210, 214, and 218. To explore this mystery and other questions, many thousands of radiohalos were measured in rocks worldwide. This was perhaps one of the largest-scale radiohalo studies ever undertaken.

The RATE research suggests that the polonium isotopes are derived from uranium via accelerated decay. The polonium atoms then were rapidly removed and transported away from their uranium sources by underground hydrothermal fluids. The polonium atoms accumulated at new sites and formed secondary radiohalos near their uranium parent halos. Thus, the short-lived isotopes are not parentless after all, but instead were physically removed from their point of origin.

4. Many rock units worldwide were analyzed by radioisotope dating techniques. These experiments include the parent-daughter isotopes potassium-argon, rubidium-strontium, samarium-neodymium, and also the lead-lead method. The efforts gave fresh data on apparent ages and their consistency. Some examples of concordance, or agreement in age were found, while many other examples showed discordance, or disagreement. In fact, both extremes often occurred for the same rock unit.

Great trust is traditionally placed in the results from isochron plots. These are graphs which are thought to give valid information on initial conditions, possible sample contamination, and sample age. The RATE results raise serious cautions concerning the interpretation of isochrons. Even when an isochron plot of data appears to produce a straight line with excellent statistical support, the calculated sample age is often in conflict with other results. The conclusion is that no isochron age can be trusted with confidence.

5. There are three important assumptions made in radioisotope dating. Each has been addressed by RATE research and found to be subject to failure. The first assumption is that the initial conditions of rock samples can be determined accurately. This is challenged by the many discordant isochron dates. Also, ancient dates are often obtained for volcanic rocks known to be very recent in origin. The second assumption is that the open or closed nature of rock samples can be determined and quantified. However, there are frequent indications of the mixing of mantle and crustal isotopes with rock samples. Also, polonium radiohalos show the movement of isotopes through rocks and minerals by hydrothermal transport. The third assumption is that nuclear half-lives have remained constant throughout history. This assumption is countered by the unexpected helium found in "ancient" zircons. Also, there are abundant radiohalos and fission tracks in rocks which were rapidly deposited during the Flood.

6. *The concept of accelerated decay arises many times in the RATE work.* It is the logical inference of placing millions or billions of year's worth of nuclear decay, at present rates, into a short time frame. The episodes of increased nuclear activity appear to have occurred during the creation week and also during the flood of Noah's day.

The evidences for vast amounts of decay include the abundance of nuclear decay products, high concentrations of helium atoms residing in zircon crystals, radiohalos, and fission tracks. Theoretical RATE studies suggest several possible ways by which nuclear decay could have been accelerated. Of special interest are large changes in decay rates that can result from a temporary adjustment of various physical constants and parameters. The ideas are rather complex and involve nuclear forces, higher dimensions, and string theory. This theoretical RATE work provides possible mechanisms for accelerated nuclear decay.

7. *The RATE radioisotope dating measurements also contribute information regarding accelerated nuclear decay.* These measurements reveal two distinct trends. First, the isotopes which decay by alpha particle emission tend to give older dates than the isotopes which undergo beta decay. Second, heavier isotopes tend to give older dates than lighter isotopes. Neither of these trends should exist if the

radioisotopes have had constant half-lives and accurately measure the ages of rocks. This decay information may provide useful clues to understanding the mechanisms responsible for accelerated nuclear decay.

8. The linguistic studies of Genesis 1:1–2:3 likewise support a recent creation. This research shows that biblical texts may be identified as either narrative or poetry with a high degree of confidence, based on the Hebrew verb forms used by the authors. The distributions of finite verbs in numerous Old Testament narrative and poetic passages were analyzed. The Genesis creation story is found to be a narrative account describing literal historical events. This conclusion challenges all efforts to explain away the early chapters of Genesis as non-literal poetry, metaphor, or allegory. The research also contradicts the currently popular idea that the Genesis account describes the big-bang theory in pre-scientific terms.

CHALLENGES FOR THE FUTURE

Skeptics of the RATE project might prefer to call this "the section of unsolved problems." It is certainly true that the RATE effort does not answer every question nor solve every problem encountered. Of course, this was never the intent of the scientists involved. The following are some of the areas which await further work, in no particular order of priority.

1. Accelerated nuclear decay involves millions or billions of years worth of decay occurring in just days or months of time. Even at present rates, considerable heat is produced by radioactive nuclear decay. An acceleration of the process will multiply the heat output greatly. This heat, which is produced within rocks, must be removed, or it could melt or even vaporize the earth's crust. This clearly did not happen to the earth. In fact, the existence of zircons within helium, radiohalos, and fission tracks shows that the host rocks and minerals have not experienced excessive heating. These physical records of nuclear decay would rapidly disappear if temperatures increased to hundreds of degrees. Possible mechanisms have been explored that could safeguard the earth from severe overheating during accelerated decay events. One of these involves cosmological or volume cooling, the result of a rapid expansion of space. Many details remain to be filled in for this and other proposed processes of heat removal.

2. *The acceleration of nuclear decay gives rise to some basic unanswered questions.* Why did it occur and what was the mechanism? Exactly when did the decay rates increase? Each of these questions has both scientific and theological components. There is also a serious concern for the protection of plant, animal, and human life from increased nuclear radiation during the Genesis flood event. Further insight is needed on these issues.

3. *The RATE project has been limited in its scope to earth materials.* However, radioisotope studies of lunar rocks and meteorites also yield ancient radioisotope ages. The youngest known lunar meteorite, found in Africa's Sahara Desert, is dated at 2.9 billion years by radioisotope methods. Several meteorites found in Antarctica and elsewhere appear to have originated from Mars. These specimens also show ages in excess of a billion years. Other key meteorites are used as indexes or standards for dating the earth and the rest of the solar system. Similar isotope information implying large-scale nuclear decay is found in the light spectra from distant stars. To explain these additional observations, the concept of accelerated decay needs to be extended to include the solar system and space beyond. Indeed, half-life alteration appears to be a cosmic or universe-wide phenomenon.

4. *The RATE age studies of various rock formations should be expanded to additional samples and geological sites.* For example, the helium retention in zircons has been explored mainly at one location, the deep borehole in New Mexico. There are countless granite samples from all around the world which are available for detailed helium analysis.

Other specific areas of new data collection and analysis would be especially helpful. Consider, for example, the trends of nuclear decay whereby alpha decay isotopes appear to give older ages than the beta decay isotopes. Also, the heavier isotopes tend to give the oldest ages for samples. These are significant results which need further verification. There are several other radioisotopes, not explored by the RATE team, which could reinforce these trends. Lutetium-hafnium and rhenium-osmium isotopes, listed in Table 2-1, are both beta emitters. Many of their isochron dating results are already available in the literature and await analysis from the young-earth creation perspective.

5. *Chapter 9 mentioned the possibility that potassium-40 might have been lacking in pre-Flood forms of life including people.* The reason is to avoid a lethal dose of internal radiation during accelerated decay events. It should be possible to investigate this idea. There are fossil organisms available whose basic makeup has been preserved without the loss of their internal chemical elements. For example, ants, beetles, caddis flies, feathers, and plant fragments are found trapped and sealed in amber. Amber is hardened resin or sap which was secreted by pine trees in the distant past. Some of these fossils may date from pre-Flood or early post-Flood times. Samples of these entombed fossils could be analyzed for their potassium-40 content if technical difficulties of such analyses could be overcome. The results would show whether historic, organic potassium-40 levels were lower than the amounts present in organisms living today.

6. *Additional, potential radioisotope research involves what are called extinct isotopes.* There are dozens of stable daughter products found in nature that are derived from radioactive parents which no longer exist in significant amounts. These "orphan" daughter isotopes are found across the earth and also in space. One particular daughter product, magnesium-26, is detected in the light spectra of stars. It is thought to result from the decay of aluminum-26, an extinct isotope

with a half-life of about 720,000 years. Other half-lives of extinct parent isotopes range from thousands to millions of years. The study of these extinct isotopes could provide additional information on the mechanisms of accelerated decay.

THE IMPACT OF RATE

The RATE results provide support for the young-earth paradigm or model for earth history. Many creation scientists in past decades laid the foundation that the RATE team has further refined and developed. Some of this new work has already been presented at professional meetings of the American Geophysical Union and the Geological Society of America. This summary book is accompanied by two technical publications and also a video production, all designed to communicate the RATE research results to a diverse audience. Other RATE public presentations and writings are underway. The RATE team does not anticipate that the young-earth creation model will overtake evolution and its broadly accepted icon of deep time in the near future. However, we are encouraged by wide popular interest in the biblical young-earth view.

The case can be made that all scientific research is actually creation research. After all, any exploration of nature is an inquiry into the details of the present-day creation. It is the interpretation of data which sometimes goes astray and conflicts with the biblical world view. It is our hope that this summary of the RATE project provides some needed balance in promoting the creation view of origins. We also hope the work will serve three major purposes. The first purpose of the RATE effort is to provide a reasoned, courteous challenge to skeptics of young-earth creation. If the earth is much younger than usually assumed, then there are many profound implications to consider. The second purpose is to encourage the millions of advocates worldwide who hold to a recent supernatural creation. Young-earth creation is neither outdated nor in opposition to science. Instead, it is a refreshing alternative to modern evolutionary assumptions. The third major purpose of RATE concerns the many students who have an intense interest in the creation world view. This includes all levels of study from elementary through post-graduate programs and beyond. In future years, some of you will greatly advance creation research. It is our hope that the RATE project will inspire your generation to advance this exciting work to new levels of scholarship and discovery.

References

Austin, Steven. 1994. *Grand Canyon: Monument to Catastrophe*. El Cajon, CA: Institute for Creation Research.

Clarke, Tom. 2003. Geologists Seek to Put an End to Blind Dates. *Nature*, 425(6958), 550–551.

DeYoung, Don. 2004. *Geology and Creation*. Chino Valley, AZ: Creation Research Society Books.

Elston, Donald P. and E.H. McKee. 1982. Age and Correlation of the Late Proterozoic Grand Canyon Disturbance, Northern Arizona. *Geological Society of America Bulletin*, 93, 681–699.

Faure, Gunter and Teresa M. Mensing. 2005. *Isotopes: Principles and Applications*. Hoboken, NJ: John Wiley and Sons.

Gentry, Robert. 1988. *Creation's Tiny Mystery*. Knoxville, TN: Earth Science Associates.

Humphreys, D. Russell. 1994. *Starlight and Time*. Green Forest, AR: Master Books.

Kerr, Richard. 1999. Tweaking the Clock of Radioactive Decay, *Science*, 286 (5441), 882–883.

Mathez, Edmond. 2004. A Birthstone for the Earth. *Natural History*, 113(4), 40–45.

Morris, Henry. 2002. *The Biblical Basis for Modern Science*. Green Forest, AR: Master Books.

Ohanian, Hans. 1985. *Physics,* Volume 2. New York: W. W. Norton and Company.

Powell, John Wesley. 1969. *The Colorado River Region* (1875), Line drawing reproduced by the U.S. Geological Survey in Professional Paper 669.

Sternberg, Meir. 1985. *The Poetics of Biblical Narrative: Ideological Literature and the Drama of Reading*. Bloomington, IN: Indiana University Press.

Vardiman, Larry, Andrew Snelling, and Eugene Chaffin, editors. 2000. *Radioisotopes and the Age of the Earth: A Young Earth Creationist Research Initiative*. El Cajon, CA: Institute for Creation Research.

Vardiman, Larry, Andrew Snelling, and Eugene Chaffin, editors. 2005. *Radioisotopes and the Age of the Earth: Results of a Young Earth Creationist Research Initiative*. El Cajon, CA: Institute for Creation Research.

Wooden, J.L., P.A. Mueller, D.K. Hunt, and D.R. Bowes. 1982. *Precambrian Geology of the Beartooth Mountains, Montana and Wyoming*, Montana Bureau of Mines and Geology Special Publication 84.

Name Index

Subject Index